NEW BOOKS AND NEW EDITIONS

PUBLISHED BY

TICKNOR, REED, AND FIELDS.

HENRY W. LONGFELLOW'S WRITINGS.

Complete Poetical Works. This edition contains the six Volumes mentioned below, and is the only complete collection in the market. In two volumes, 16mo, $2.00.

In separate Volumes, each 75 cents.

VOICES OF THE NIGHT.
BALLADS and OTHER POEMS.
SPANISH STUDENT; A Play in Three Acts.
BELFRY OF BRUGES and OTHER POEMS.
EVANGELINE; a Tale of Acadie.
THE SEASIDE AND THE FIRESIDE.
THE WAIF. A Collection of Poems. Edited by Longfellow.
THE ESTRAY. A Collection of Poems. Edited by Longfellow.

MR. LONGFELLOW'S PROSE WORKS.

Hyperion. A Romance. In one volume, 16mo, price $1.00.

Outre-Mer. A Pilgrimage Beyond the Sea. In one volume, 16mo, price $1.00.

Kavanagh. A Tale. Lately published. In one vol. 16mo, price 75 cents.

NATHANIEL HAWTHORNE'S WRITINGS.

Twice-Told Tales. A New Edition. In two vols. 16mo, with Portrait, price $1.50.

The Scarlet Letter. A Romance. In one vol. 16mo, price 75 cents.

The House of the Seven Gables. In one volume, 16mo, price $1.00.

True Stories from History and Biography. In one volume, 16mo, with fine Engravings, price 75 cents.

JOHN G. WHITTIER'S WRITINGS.

OLD PORTRAITS AND MODERN SKETCHES. In one vol. 16mo. Just published, price 75 cents.

MARGARET SMITH'S JOURNAL. In one volume, 16mo, price 75 cents cloth, 50 cents in paper.

SONGS OF LABOR AND OTHER POEMS. In one volume, 16mo, price 50 cents.

OLIVER WENDELL HOLMES'S WRITINGS.

POEMS. In one volume, 16mo. New Edition, enlarged, with fine Portrait. Price $1.00.

ASTRÆA, THE BALANCE OF ILLUSIONS. In one vol. 16mo, price 25 cents.

ALFRED TENNYSON'S WRITINGS.

POEMS. A New Edition, enlarged, with Portrait. In two volumes, 16mo, price $1.50.

THE PRINCESS. A Medley. In one volume, 16mo, price 50 cents.

IN MEMORIAM. In one volume, 16mo, price 75 cents.

THOMAS DE QUINCEY'S WRITINGS.

CONFESSIONS OF AN ENGLISH OPIUM-EATER AND SUSPIRIA DE PROFUNDIS. In one volume, 16mo, price 75 cents.

BIOGRAPHICAL ESSAYS. In one volume, 16mo, price 75 cents.

MISCELLANEOUS ESSAYS. In one volume, 16mo, price 75 cents.

THE CÆSARS. In one volume, 16mo, price 75 cents.

GRACE GREENWOOD'S WRITINGS.

GREENWOOD LEAVES. A Collection of Stories and Letters. In one volume, 12mo. New Edition, price $1.25.

POEMS. In one volume, 16mo, with fine Portrait. Price 75 cents.

HISTORY OF MY PETS. A Book for Children. With fine Engravings. Price 50 cents.

EDWIN P. WHIPPLE'S WRITINGS.

ESSAYS AND REVIEWS. A New and Revised edition. In two volumes, 16mo, price $2.00.

LECTURES ON SUBJECTS CONNECTED WITH LITERATURE AND LIFE. In one volume, 16mo, price 63 cents.

WASHINGTON AND THE REVOLUTION. In one volume, 16mo, price 20 cents.

HENRY GILES'S WRITINGS.

LECTURES, ESSAYS, AND MISCELLANEOUS WRITINGS. Two volumes, 16mo, price $1 50.

CHRISTIAN THOUGHT ON LIFE. In Twelve Discourses. In one volume, 16mo, price 75 cents.

WILLIAM MOTHERWELL'S WRITINGS.

POEMS, NARRATIVE AND LYRICAL. A New Edition, Enlarged. In one volume, 16mo, price 75 cents.

POSTHUMOUS POEMS. In one volume, 16mo, price 50 cents.

MINSTRELSY, ANCIENT AND MODERN. In two vols. 16mo, price $1.50.

JAMES RUSSELL LOWELL'S WRITINGS.

COMPLETE POETICAL WORKS. Revised, with Additions. In two volumes, 16mo, price $1.50.

MISCELLANEOUS.

CHARLES SPRAGUE. POETICAL AND PROSE WRITINGS. With fine Portrait. In one volume, 16mo, price 75 cents.

JOHN G. SAXE. HUMOROUS AND SATIRICAL POEMS. In one volume, 16mo, price 50 cents.

ROBERT BROWNING. COMPLETE POETICAL WORKS. In two volumes, 16mo, price $2.00.

BARRY CORNWALL. ENGLISH SONGS AND OTHER SMALL POEMS. Enlarged Edition. In one volume, 16mo, $1 00.

RICHARD MONCKTON MILNES. POEMS OF MANY YEARS. In one volume, 16mo, price 75 cents.

THE SOLITARY OF JUAN FERNANDEZ; OR, THE REAL ROBINSON CRUSOE. By the Author of Picciola. One volume, 16mo, price 50 cents.

WILLIAM WORDSWORTH'S BIOGRAPHY. By Dr. C. WORDSWORTH. Edited by Prof. HENRY REED. Two volumes, 16mo, price $2.50.

GOETHE'S WILHELM MEISTER. Translated by CARLYLE. In two volumes, 16mo, price $2 50.

GOETHE'S FAUST. Translated by HAYWARD. In one volume, 16mo. New Edition, price 75 cents.

CHARLES SUMNER. ORATIONS AND SPEECHES. In two volumes, 16mo, price $2.50.

GEORGE S. HILLARD. THE DANGERS AND DUTIES OF THE MERCANTILE PROFESSION. In one volume, 16mo, price 25 cents.

HORACE MANN. A FEW THOUGHTS FOR A YOUNG MAN. In one volume, 16mo, price 25 cents.

HENRY T. TUCKERMAN. POEMS. In one volume, 16mo, price 75 cents.

PHILLIP JAMES BAILEY. THE ANGEL WORLD AND OTHER POEMS. In one volume, 16mo, price 50 cents.

F. W. P. GREENWOOD. SERMONS OF CONSOLATION. In one volume, 16mo, price $1.00.

MEMORY AND HOPE. A BOOK OF POEMS, REFERRING TO CHILDHOOD. In one volume, 8vo, price $2.00.

REJECTED ADDRESSES. By HORACE and JAMES SMITH. In one volume, 16mo, price 50 cents.

WARRENIANA. By the Authors of Rejected Addresses. In one volume, 16mo, price 75 cents.

ALDERBROOK. By FANNY FORESTER. In two vols. 12mo, price $1.75.

THE BOSTON BOOK. BEING SPECIMENS OF METROPOLITAN LITERATURE. In one volume, 12mo, price $1.25.

HEROINES OF THE MISSIONARY ENTERPRISE. In one volume, 16mo, price 75 cents.

ANGEL-VOICES; or WORDS OF COUNSEL FOR OVERCOMING THE WORLD. In one volume, 18mo, price 38 cents.

MEMOIR OF THE BUCKMINSTERS, FATHER AND SON. By MRS. LEE. In one volume, 12mo.

EACH OF THE ABOVE POEMS AND PROSE WRITINGS, MAY BE HAD IN VARIOUS STYLES OF HANDSOME BINDING.

MOTHERWELL'S

POSTHUMOUS POEMS.

The American Publishers have issued this volume in uniform style with their other editions of the Writings of Motherwell, in order that the series might be complete. The volumes already published comprise the *Poetical Works* with the *Memoir*, and the *Minstrelsy, Ancient* and *Modern*.

POSTHUMOUS POEMS

OF

WILLIAM MOTHERWELL.

NOW FIRST COLLECTED.

BOSTON:
TICKNOR, REED, AND FIELDS.
MDCCCLI.

THURSTON, TORRY, AND EMERSON, PRINTERS.

PREFACE TO THE GLASGOW EDITION.

When the Second Edition of Motherwell's Poems was published, in 1847, it was stated in the Preface that the fragments of poetry which he had left behind him in manuscript, and which were not included in that volume, might be given to the public at some future day, should any encouragement be offered for pursuing such a course. This the Publisher has now determined to do; but before taking such a step, he resolved to submit the pieces in question to the critical scrutiny of Motherwell's old friend and poetical ally, Mr. William Kennedy, who chanced to be in Scotland at the time. The reader will, therefore, be good enough to understand that these Poems have been selected by Mr. Kennedy, and are published under his express authority. The Publisher is gratified in being able to make this statement, as it relieves him from a responsibility which he feels that it would not be becoming in him to incur.

LINES

Written after a Visit to the Grave of my Friend,

WILLIAM MOTHERWELL,

NOVEMBER, 1847.

PLACE we a stone at his head and his feet;
Sprinkle his sward with the small flowers sweet;
Piously hallow the Poet's retreat!
    Ever approvingly,
    Ever most lovingly,
Turned he to Nature, a worshipper meet.

Harm not the thorn which grows at his head;
Odorous honors its blossoms will shed,
Grateful to him, early summoned, who sped
    Hence, not unwillingly —
    For he felt thrillingly —
To rest his poor heart 'mong the low-lying dead.

Dearer to him than the deep Minster bell,
Winds of sad cadence, at midnight, will swell,
Vocal with sorrows he knoweth too well,
    Who, for the early day,
    Plaining this roundelay,
Might his own fate from a brother's foretell.

Worldly ones treading this terrace of graves,
Grudge not the minstrel the little he craves,
When o'er the snow-mound the winter-blast raves —
          Tears — which devotedly,
          Though all unnotedly,
Flow from their spring, in the soul's silent caves.

Dreamers of noble thoughts, raise him a shrine,
Graced with the beauty which lives in his line;
Strew with pale flow'rets, when pensive moons shine,
          His grassy covering,
          Where spirits hovering,
Chaunt, for his requiem, music divine.

Not as a record he lacketh a stone!
Pay a light debt to the singer we've known —
Proof that our love for his name hath not flown
          With the frame perishing —
          That we are cherishing
Feelings akin to the lost Poet's own.

William Kennedy.

CONTENTS.

POEMS.

POSTHUMOUS POEMS.

O THAT THIS WEARY WAR OF LIFE!

O THAT this weary war of life
With me were o'er,
Its eager cry of wo and strife
Heard never more!
I've fronted the red battle field
Mine own dark day;
I fain would fling the helmet, shield,
And sword away.
I strive not now for victory —
That wish hath fled;
My prayer is now to numbered be
Among the dead —
All that I loved, alas! — alas!
Hath perished!

They tell me 'tis a glorious thing,
    This wearing war;
They tell me joy crowns suffering
    And bosom scar.
Such speech might never pass the lips
    That could unfold
How shrinketh heart when sorrow nips
    Affections old:
When they who cleaved to us are dust,
    Why live to moan?
Better to meet a felon thrust
    Than strive alone —
Better than loveless palaces
    The churchyard stone!

CHOICE OF DEATH.

Might I, without offending, choose
  The death that I would die,
I'd fall, as erst the Templar fell,
  Aneath a Syrian sky.

Upon a glorious plain of war,
  The banners floating fair,
My lance and fluttering pennoncel
  Should marshal heroes there!

Upon the solemn battle-eve,
  With prayer to be forgiven,
I'd arm me for a righteous fight,
  Imploring peace of Heaven!

High o'er the thunders of the charge
  Should wave my sable plume,
And where the day was lost or won,
  There should they place my tomb!

LIKE MIST ON A MOUNTAIN TOP BROKEN AND GRAY.

LIKE mist on a mountain top broken and gray,
The dream of my early day fleeted away:
Now the evening of life, with its shadows, steals on,
And memory reposes on years that are gone!

Wild youth with strange fruitage of errors and tears —
A midday of bliss and a midnight of fears —
Though chequer'd, and sad, and mistaken you've been,
Still love I to muse on the hours we have seen!

With those long-vanished hours fair visions are flown,
And the soul of the minstrel sinks pensive and lone;
In vain would I ask of the future to bring
The verdure that gladden'd my life in its spring!

I think of the glen where the hazle-nut grew—
The pine-covered hill where the heather-bell blew—
The trout-burn which soothed with its murmuring
sweet,
The wild flowers that gleamed on the red deer's re-
treat!

I look for the mates full of ardour and truth,
Whose joys, like my own, were the sunbeams of
youth—
They passed ere the morning of hope knew its close—
They left me to sleep where our fathers repose!

Where is now the wide hearth with the big faggot's
blaze,
Where circled the legend and song of old days?
The legend's forgotten, the hearth is grown cold,
The home of my childhood to strangers is sold!

Like a pilgrim who speeds on a perilous way,
I pause, ere I part, oft again to survey
Those scenes ever dear to the friends I deplore,
Whose feast of young smiles I may never share more!

SONG.

If to thy heart I were as near
  As thou art near to mine,
I'd hardly care though a' the year
Nae sun on earth suld shine, my dear,
  Nae sun on earth suld shine!

Twin starnies are thy glancin' een —
  A warld they'd licht and mair —
And gin that ye be my Christine,
Ae blink to me ye'll spare, my dear,
  Ae blink to me ye'll spare!

My leesome May I've wooed too lang —
  Aneath the trystin' tree,
I've sung till a' the plantins rang,
Wi' lays o' love for thee, my dear,
  Wi' lays o' love for thee.

The dew-draps glisten on the green,
  The laverocks lilt on high,
We 'll forth and doun the loan, Christine,
And kiss when nane is nigh, my dear,
  And kiss when nane is nigh !

TRUE WOMAN.

No quaint conceit of speech,
  No golden, minted phrase —
Dame Nature needs to teach
  To echo Woman's praise;
Pure love and truth unite
To do thee, Woman, right!

She is the faithful mirror
  Of thoughts that brightest be —
Of feelings without error,
  Of matchless constancie;
When art essays to render
  More glorious Heaven's bow —
To paint the virgin splendour
  Of fresh-fallen mountain snow —
New fancies will I find,
To laud true Woman's mind.

No words can lovelier make
  Virtue's all-lovely name,
No change can ever shake
  A woman's virtuous fame:
The moon is forth anew,
  Though envious clouds endeavour
To screen her from our view —
  More beautiful than ever:
So, through detraction's haze,
True Woman shines alwaies.

The many-tinted rose,
  Of gardens is the queen,
The perfumed Violet knows
  No peer where she is seen
The flower of woman-kind
Is aye a gentle mind.

FRIENDSHIP AND LOVE.

Oft have I sighed for pleasure past,
  Oft wept for secret smarting —
But far the heaviest drop of all
That ever on my cheek did fall
  The tear was at our parting.

Why did our bosoms ever beat
  Harmonious with each other,
If truest sympathies of soul
Might broken be, perhaps the whole
  Concentred in another?

My fear it was when other scenes,
  With other tongues, and faces,
Should greet thee, thou would'st haply be
Forgetful of our amity
  In old frequented places.

'T is even so — the thrall of love,
  Past ties to thee seem common —
Well, hearts *must* yield to beauty rare,
And proud-souled friendship hardly dare
  Contest the prize with woman!

Old friend, adieu! I blame thee not,
  Since fair guest fills thy bosom —
Thy smiling love may flattered be
Our bonds to know, and feel that she
  Thy pow'r had to unloose them!

Since thou surrenderest all for her,
  May she, with faith unshaken,
Place every thought on thee alone,
While he who Friendship's dream hath known,
  Must from that dream awaken!

AND HAE YE SEEN MY AIN TRUE LUVE?

'And hae ye seen my ain true luve
As ye cam thro' the fair?
Ae blink o' her 's worth a' the goud
And gear that glistens there!'—
'And how suld I ken your true luve
Frae ither lasses braw
That trysted there, busked out like queens,
Wi' pearlins knots and a'?'

'Ye may ken her by her snaw-white skin,
And by her waist sae sma';
Ye may ken her by her searchin' ee,
And hair like glossy craw;
Ye may ken her by the hinnie mou,
And by the rose-dyed cheek,
But best o' a' by smiles o' licht
That luve's ain language speak!

'Ye may ken her by her fairy step—
As she trips up the street,
The very pavement seems to shine
Aneath her genty feet!
Ye may ken her by the jewell'd rings
Upon her fingers sma',
Yet better by the dignity
That she glides through them a'.

'And ye may ken her by the voice—
The music o' her tongue—
Wha heard her speak incontinent
Wad think an angel sung!
And such seems she to me, and mair,
That wale o' woman's charms—
It's bliss to press her dear wee mou
And daut her in my arms!'

THE SPELL-BOUND KNIGHT.

Lady, dar'st thou seek the shore
Which ne'er woman's footstep bore;—
Where beneath yon rugged steep,
Restless rolls the darksome deep?

Dar'st thou, though thy blood run chill,
Thither speed at midnight still—
And when horror rules the sky,
Raise for lover lost thy cry?

Dar'st thou at that ghastiest hour
Breathe the word of magic power—
Word that breaks the mermaid's spell,
Which false lover knows too well?

When affrighted spectres rise
'Twixt pale floods and ebon skies,
Dar'st thou, reft of maiden fear,
Bid the Water-Witch appear?

When upon the sallow tide
Pearly elfin boat does glide,
When the mystic oar is heard,
Like the wing of baleful bird —
Dar'st thou with a voice of might
Call upon thy spell-bound knight?

When the shallop neareth land,
Dar'st thou, with thy snow-white hand,
Boldly on the warrior's breast
Place the Cross by Churchman blest? —
When is done this work of peril,
Thou hast won proud Ulster's Earl!

CRUXTOUN CASTLE.

The reader will find a brief, but instructive, account of this relic of Baronial times — which, at different periods, has been written Cruxtoun, Croestoun, and Crookston — in a work entitled 'Views in Renfrewshire,' by Philip A. Ramsay, one of the Poet's earliest and truest friends. Of the objects of antiquity remaining in Renfrewshire, Cruxtoun Castle, according to Mr. Ramsay, is, in point of interest, second only to the Abbey of Paisley. 'The ruins of this castle,' he observes, 'occupy the summit of a wooded slope, overhanging the south bank of the White Cart, about three miles south-east from Paisley, and close to the spot where that river receives the waters of a stream called the Levern. The scenery in this neighbourhood is rich and varied, and although the eminence on which the Castle stands is but gentle, it is so commanding that our great Novelist has made Queen Mary remark, that "from thence you may see a prospect wide as from the peaks of Schehallion." To Cruxtoun Castle, then the property of Darnley, Mary's husband, tradition tells us, the royal bride was conducted, soon after the celebration of their nuptials at Edinburgh.'

Thou grey and antique tower,
Receive a wanderer of the lonely night,
Whose moodful sprite
Rejoices at this witching time to brood

Amid thy shattered strength's dim solitude!
It is a fear-fraught hour —
A death-like stillness reigns around,
Save the wood-skirted river's eerie sound,
And the faint rustling of the trees that shower
Their brown leaves on the stream,
Mournfully gleaming in the moon's pale beam:
O! I could dwell for ever and for ever
In such a place as this, with such a night!
When, o'er thy waters and thy waving woods,
The moon-beams sympathetically quiver,
And no ungentle thing on thee intrudes,
And every voice is dumb, and every object bright!
Forgive, old Cruxtoun, if, with step unholy,
Unwittingly a pilgrim should profane
The regal quiet, the august repose,
Which o'er thy desolated summit reign —
When the fair moon's abroad, at evening's close —
Or interrupt that touching melancholy —
Image of fallen grandeur — softly thrown
O'er every crumbling and moss-bedded stone,
And broken arch, and pointed turret hoar,
Which speak a tale of times that are no more;
Of triumphs they have seen,
When Minstrel-craft, in praise of Scotland's Queen,
Woke all the magic of the harp and song,

3

And the rich, varied, and fantastic lore
Of those romantic days was carped, I ween,
Amidst the pillared pomp of lofty hall,
By many a jewelled throng
Of smiling dames and soldier barons bold;
When the loud cheer of generous wassail rolled
From the high deis to where the warder strode,
Proudly, along the battlemented wall,
Beneath his polished armour's ponderous load;
Who paused to hear, and carolled back again,
With martial glee, the jocund vesper strain:
Thou wilt forgive! Mine is no peering eye,
That seeks, with glance malign, the suffering part,
Thereby, with hollow show of sympathy,
To smite again the poor world-wounded heart:
No — thy misfortunes win from him a sigh
Whose soul towers, like thyself, o'er each lewd
passer-by.

Relique of earlier days,
Yes, dear thou art to me! —
And beauteous, marvellously,
The moon-light strays
Where banners glorious floated on thy walls —
Clipping their ivied honours with its thread
Of half-angelick light:

And though o'er thee Time's wasting dews have shed
Their all consuming blight,
Maternal moon-light falls
On and around thee full of tenderness,
Yielding thy shattered frame pure love's divine caress.

Ah me! thy joy of youthful lustyhood
Is gone, old Cruxtoun! Ever, ever gone!
Here hast thou stood
In nakedness and sorrow, roofless, lone,
For many a weary year — and to the storm
Hast bared thy wasted form —
Braving destruction, in the attitude
Of reckless desolation. Like to one
Who in this world no longer may rejoice,
Who watching by Hope's grave
With stern delight, impatient is to brave
The worst of coming ills — So, Cruxtoun! thou
Rear'st to the tempest thy undaunted brow;
When Heaven's red coursers flash athwart the sky —
Startling the guilty as they thunder by —
Then raisest thou a wild, unearthly hymn,
Like death-desiring bard whose star hath long been dim!

Neglected though thou art,
Sad remnant of old Scotland's worthier days,

When independence had its chivalrie,
There still is left one heart
To mourn for thee!
And though, alas! thy venerable form
Must bide the buffet of each vagrant storm,
One spirit yet is left to linger here
And pay the tribute of a silent tear;
Who in his memory registers the dints
That Time hath graved upon thy sorrowing brow;
Who of thy woods loves the Autumnal tints,
Whose voice — perforce indignant — mingles now
In all thy lamentations — with the tone,
Not of these paltry times, but of brave years long gone.

Nor is't the moonshine clear,
Leeming on tower, and tree, and silent stream,
Nor hawthorn blossoms which in Spring appear,
Most prodigal of perfume — nor the sweets
Of wood-flowers, peeping up at the blue sky;
Nor the mild aspect of blue hills which greet
The eager vision — blessed albeit they seem,
Each with its charm particular — To my eye,
Old Cruxtoun hath an interest all its own —
From many a cherished, intersociate thought —
From feelings multitudinous well known
To souls in whom the patriot fire hath wrought

Sublime remembrance of their country's fame:
Radiant thou art in the ethereal flame—
The lustrous splendour—which those feelings shed
O'er many a scene of this my father-land!
Thou, grey magician, with thy potent wand,
Evok'st the shades of the illustrious dead!
The mists dissolve—up rise the slumbering years—
On come the knightly riders cap-a-pie—
The herald calls—hark, to the clash of spears!
To Beauty's Queen each hero bends the knee;
Dreams of the Past, how exquisite ye be—
Offspring of heavenly faith and rare antiquity!

Light feet have trod
The soft, green, flowering sod
That girdles thy baronial strength, and traced,
All gracefully, the labyrinthine dance;
Young hearts discoursed with many a passionate glance,
While rose and fell the Minstrel's thrilling strain—
(Who, in this iron age, might sing in vain—
His largesse coarse neglect, and mickle pain!)
Waste are thy chambers tenantless, which long
Echoed the notes of gleeful minstrelsie—
Notes once the prelude to a tale of wrong,
Of Royalty and love.—Beneath yon tree—
Now bare and blasted—so our annals tell—

The martyr Queen, ere that her fortunes knew
A darker shade than cast her favourite yew,
Loved Darnley passing well —
Loved him with tender woman's generous love,
And bade farewell awhile to courtly state
And pageantry for yon o'ershadowing grove —
For the lone river's banks where small birds sing —
Their little hearts with summer joys elate —
Where tall broom blossoms, flowers profusely spring;
There he, the most exalted of the land,
Pressed, with the grace of youth, a Sovereign's peer-
less hand.

And she did die! —
Die as a traitor — in the brazen gaze
Of her — a kinswoman and enemy —
O well may such an act my soul amaze!
My country, at that hour, where slept thy sword?
Where was the high and chivalrous accord,
To fling the avenging banner of our land,
Like sheeted flame, forth to the winds of heaven?
O shame among the nations — thus to brook
The damning stain to thy escutcheon given!
How could thy sons upon their mothers look,
Degenerate Scotland! heedless of the wail
Of thy lorn Queen, in her captivity!

Unmov'd wert thou by all her bitter bale —
Untouch'd by thought that she had governed thee —
Hard was each heart and cold each powerful hand —
No harnessed steed rushed panting to the fight;
O listless fell the lance when Mary laid
Her head upon the block — and high in soul,
Which lacked not then thy frugal sympathy,
Died — in her widowed beauty, penitent —
Whilst thou, by foul red-handed faction rent,
Wert falsest recreant to sweet majesty!

'T is past — she rests — the scaffold hath been swept,
The headsman's guilty axe to rust consigned —
But, Cruxtoun, while thine aged towers remain,
And thy green umbrage wooes the evening wind —
By noblest natures shall her woes be wept,
Who shone the glory of thy festal day:
Whilst aught is left of these thy ruins grey,
They will arouse remembrance of the stain
Queen Mary's doom hath left on History's page —
Remembrance laden with reproach and pain,
To those who make, like me, this pilgrimage!

ROLAND AND ROSABELLE.

A tomb by skilful hands is raised,
  Close to a sainted shrine,
And there is laid a stalwart Knight,
  The last of all his line.
Beside that noble monument,
  A Squire doth silent stand,
Leaning in pensive wise upon
  The cross-hilt of his brand.

Around him peals the harmony
  Of friars at even-song,
He notes them not, as passing by
  The hymning brothers throng:
And he hath watched the monument
  Three weary nights and days,
And ever on the marble cold
  Is fixed his steadfast gaze.

'I pray thee, wakeful Squire, unfold'—
 Proud Rosabella said—
'The story of the warrior bold,
 Who in this tomb is laid!'
'A champion of the Cross was he'—
 The Squire made low reply—
'And on the shore of Galilee,
 In battle did he die.

'He bound me by a solemn vow,
 His body to convey
Where lived his love—there rests it now,
 Until the judgment-day:
And by his stone of record here,
 In loyalty I stand,
Until I greet his leman dear—
 The Lady of the Land!'

'Fair stranger, I would learn of thee
 The gentle warrior's name,
Who fighting fell at Galilee
 And won a deathless name?'
The Squire hath fixed an eye of light
 Full on the Lady tall—
'Men called,' he said, 'that hapless Knight
 Sir Roland of the Hall!

'His foot was foremost in the fray,
And last to leave the field —
A braver arm in danger's day
Ne'er shivered lance on shield!'
'In death, what said he of his love —
Thou faithful soldier tell?'
'Meekly he prayed to Him above
For perjured Rosabelle.'

'Thy task is done — my course is run —
(O fast her tears did fall!)
I am indeed a perjured one —
Dear Roland of the Hall!'
Even as the marble cold and pale,
Waxed Rosabella's cheek;
The faithful Squire resumed travail —
The Lady's heart did break!

SONG.

How I envy the ring that encircles thy finger! —
  Dear daughter of beauty how happy were I
If, by some sweet spell, like that ring, I might linger
  At ease in the light of thy heart-thrilling eye!

I would joy in the music thy light pulse is making,
  I would press the soft cheek where the rose-buds unfold —
I would rest on the brow where pure thought's ever waking,
  And lovingly glide through thy tresses of gold.

On the ripe smiling lip which young Cupid is steeping
  In dews of love's day-dawn, I'd tenderly play —
And when in thy innocence, sweet, thou wert sleeping,
  I'd watch thee, and bless thee, and guard thee for aye!

FOR BLITHER FIELDS AND BRAVER BOWERS.

For blither fields and braver bowers
  The little bird, in Spring,
Quits its old tree and wintry hold,
  With wanton mates to sing;
And yet a while that wintry home
  To branch and twig may cling;
But wayward blast, or truant boy,
  May rend it soon away,
And scatter to the heedless winds
  The toil of many a day —
And where, when Winter comes, shall then
  The bird its poor head lay?

The moss, the down, the twisted grass,
  The slender wands that bound
The dear warm nest, are parted now,
  Or scattered far around —
Belike the woodman's axe hath felled
  The old tree to the ground!

And now keen Winter's wreathing snows
  O'er frozen nature lie —
The sun forgets to warm the earth,
  Forgets to light the sky ;
I fear me lest the wandering bird
  May, houseless, shivering, die !

Forgive me, Helen — thou art free
  To keep, or quit, the nest
I built for thee, and sheltered in
  The foliage of my breast,
And fenced so well none other might
  Be harbour'd there as guest.
Flee if thou wilt — if other love
  Thy fickle heart enfold,
Thou 'rt free to rove where fancy waves
  Her wand of fairy gold —
But Helen, ere thou canst return,
  This bosom will be cold !

HOPE AND LOVE.

Through life on journeying, by its thorny paths,
Or pleasant ways — its rank green hemlock wastes,
Or roseate bowers — in utter loneliness,
Or 'mid the din of busy multitudes —
Two babes of beauty linger near us still —
Twin cherubim — that leave us not until
We 've passed the threshold of that crowded inn
Which borders on Eternity! One doth point,
With gleaming eye and finger tremulous,
To clefts in azure, where the sunbeams slumber
On couch of vermeil dye and amethyst,
Bordered with flowers that never know decay;
Where living fountains, cool and argentine,
Trill on in measured cadence, night and morn:
The other, with an eye of sweet regard,
And voice the spirit of pure melody,
Sheds o'er the darkest track some ray of gladness —
To elevate the heart, and nerve the soul,
With unslacked sinews, vigorously to brave
The perils of the unattempted road:

Love, gentle Love — one fellow-pilgrim is —
The other Hope — dear, never-dying Hope! —
And they to churle, as well as keysour yield
The tender ministering of faithful friends!

SONGE OF THE SCHIPPE.

WHEN surly windes and grewsome cloudes
Are tilting in the skye,
And every little star 's abed,
That glimmered cheerilie —
O then 'tis meet for mariners
To steer righte carefulie !
For mermaides sing the schippman's dirge,
Where ocean weddes the skye —
A blessing on our gude schippe as lustilie she sailes,
O what can match our gude schippe when blest with favouring gales !

Blythely to the tall top-mast,
Up springs the sailor boy —
Could he but hail a distant port,
How he would leap with joy !
By bending yard and rope he swings —
A fair-haired child of glee —

But oh! a cruel sawcie wave
  Hath swept him in the sea!
There's sadness in the gude schippe that breasts the waters wild,
Though safe ourselves, we'll think with tears of our poor ocean-child!

Our main-mast now is clean cut downe,
  The tackle torn away —
And thundering o'er the stout schippe's side,
  The seas make fearful play!
Yet cheerlie cheerlie on we go,
  Though fierce the tempest raves,
We know the hand unseen that guides
  The schippe o'er stormie waves!
We'll all still stand by the old schippe as should a trusty crew,
For He who rules the wasting waves may some port bring to view!

Our gude schippe is a shapely schippe —
  A shapely and a stronge —
Our hearts sang to our noble schippe,
  As she careered along!
And fear ye not my sturdy mates
  Though sayles and masts be riven —

We know, while drifting o'er the deep,
Above there's still a haven!
Though sorely we're benighted upon the weltering foam,
The sun may rise upon the morn and guide us to a home!

HE STOOD ALONE.

He stood alone in an unpitying crowd —
His mates fell from him, as the grub-worms drop
From the green stalk that once had nourished them,
But now is withered and all rottenness
Because it gave such shelter. Pleasure's train —
The light-winged tribes that seek the sunshine only —
No more endeavoured from his eye to win
The smile of approbation. Grief and Care
Stalked forth upon the theatre of his heart,
In many a gloomy and mishapen guise,
Till of the glories of his earlier self
The world, his base and hollow auditory,
Left but a ghastly phantom. As a tree,
A goodly tree — that stricken is and wasted,
By elemental conflicts — falls at last,
Even in the fulness of its branching honours,
Prostrate before the storm — yet majestic
In its huge downfal, so, at last, fell he!

CUPID'S BANISHMENTE.

WHAT recke I now of comely dame?
  What care I now for fair pucelle?
Unscorchde I meet their glance of flame,
  Unmovede I mark their bosoms swel,
  For Love and I have sayde farewel!

Go, prattlynge fool! — go, wanton wilde!
  Seke thy fond mother this to tel —
That loveliest maydes on me have smyled,
  And that I stoutly did rebel,
  And bade thee and thy arts farewel!

With me thy tyrant reigne is o'er,
  Thou hear'st thy latest warninge knel;
Speed, waywarde urchin, from my doore,—
  My hert to thee gives no handsel,
  For thou and I have sworne farewel!

So trimme thy bow, and fleche thy shafte,
  And peer where sillie gallants dwel,
On them essaye thy archer crafte,
  No more on me thy bolte schal tel —
  False Love and I have sunge farewel!

THE SHIP OF THE DESERT.

'ONWARD, my Camel! — On, though slow;
Halt not upon these fatal sands!
Onward my constant Camel go —
The fierce Simoom hath ceased to blow,
We soon shall tread green Syria's lands!

'Droop not my faithful Camel! Now
The hospitable well is near!
Though sick at heart, and worn in brow,
I grieve the most to think that thou
And I may part, kind comrade, here!

'O'er the dull waste a swelling mound —
A verdant paradise — I see;
The princely date-palms there abound,
And springs that make it sacred ground
To pilgrims like to thee and me!'

The patient Camel's filmy eye,
  All lustreless, is fixed in death!
Beneath the sun of Araby
The desert wanderer ceased to sigh,
  Exhausted on its burning path.

Then rose upon the Wilderness
  The solitary Driver's cry:
Thoughts of his home upon him press,
As, in his utter loneliness,
  He sees his burden-bearer die.

Hope gives no echo to his call—
  Ne'er from his comrade will he sever!
The red sky is his funeral pall;
A prayer—a moan—'t is over, all—
  Camel and lord now rest for ever!

A three hour's journey from the spring
  Loved of the panting Caravan—
Within a little sandy ring—
The Camel's bones lie whitening,
  With thine, old, unlamented man!

THE POET'S WISH.

O WOULD that in some wild and winding glen
  Where human footstep ne'er did penetrate,
And from the haunts of base and selfish men
  Remote, in dreamy loneness situate,
I had my dwelling: and within my ken
  Nature disporting in fantastic form —
  Asleep in green repose, and thundering in the storm!

Then mine should be a life of deep delight, —
  Rare undulations of ecstatic musing;
Thoughts calm, yet ever-varying, stream bedight
  With flowers immortal of quick Fancy's choosing—
And like unto the ray of tremulous light,
  Blent by the pale moon with the entranced water,
  I'd wed thee, Solitude, dear Nature's first-born daughter!

ISABELLE.

A SERENADE.

HARK! sweet Isabelle, hark to my lute,
As softly it plaineth o'er
The story of one to whose lowly suit
Thy heart shall beat no more!
List to its tender plaints, my love,
Sad as the accents of saints, my love,
Who mortal sin deplore!

Awake from your slumber, Isabelle, wake,
'T is sorrow that tunes these strings;
A last farewell would the minstrel take
Of her whose beauty he sings:
The moon seems to weep on her way, my love,
And, shrouded in clouds, seems to say, my love,
No hope with the morning springs!

Deep on the breeze peals the hollow sound
  Of the dreary convent bell;
Its walls, ere a few short hours wheel round,
  Will girdle my Isabelle!
They'll take thee away from these arms, love,
And bury thy blossoming charms, love,
  Where midnight requiems swell.

At the high altar I see thee kneel,
  With pallid and awe-struck face;
I see the veil those looks conceal
  That shone with surpassing grace —
The shade will prey on thy bloom, my love,
While I shall wend to the tomb, my love,
  And leave of my name no trace.

We lov'd and we grew, we grew and we lov'd,
  Twin flowers in a dewy vale;
The churchman's cold hand hath one remov'd,
  The other will soon wax pale:
O fast will be its decline, my love,
As this dying note of mine, my love,
  Lost in the evening gale!

WHAT IS THIS WORLD TO ME?

What is this world to me?
A harp sans melodie;
A dream of vain idlesse,
A thought of bitterness,
That grieves the aching brain,
And gnaws the heart in twain!

My spirit pines alwaie,
Like captive shut from day;
Or like a sillie flower,
Estranged from sun and shower—
Which, withering, soon must die,
In love-lorne privacie.

No joye my hearte doth finde,
With those they calle my kinde;
O dull it is and sad,
To see how men waxe bad:
As Autumn leaves decay,
So verteue fades away!

TO A LADY'S BONNET.

Invidious shade! why thus presume,
O'er face so fair to cast thy gloom;
And hide from the enamoured sight,
Those lips so sweet and eyes so bright?
Why veil those blushes of the cheek,
Which purity of soul bespeak?
Why shroud that brow in hermit cell,
On which high thoughts serenely dwell?
Why chain severe the clustering hair,
That whilome shed a radiance rare —
A golden mist — o'er neck and brow,
Like sunset over drifted snow?

O kindly shade, for ever be
Between me and love's witchery!
For ever be to Ellen's eyes,
Like grateful cloud in summer skies,

Mellowing the fervour of the day :
For should they dart another ray
Of their enchanting light on me,
Farewell the proud boast — I am free !

THE WANDERER.

No face I look upon doth greet me
  With smile that generous welcome lends ;
No ready hand, with cheerful glow,
  Is now stretched out, all glad, to meet me :
A chill distrust on every brow,
  Assures me I have here no friends !

I miss the music of home voices,
  The rushing of the mountain flood,
My country's birds that blithely sung
  In woodlands where green May rejoices,
Discoursing love when life was young,
  And mirthful ever was my mood.

The breezes soft that fan my cheek,
  The bower that shades the sun from me,
The sky that spans this Southern shore,
  Do all a different language speak
From breeze and bower I loved of yore,
  And sky that spans my own countree.

They bring not health to exiled men —
  They light not up the home-bent eye ;
No, piece-meal wastes the way-worn frame
  That longs to tread its native glen —
That trembles when it hears the name
  Of that land where its fathers lie !

The sun which shines seems not the sun
  That rose upon my native fields ;
Majestic rolls he on his way,
  A cloudless course hath he to run —
But beams he with the kindly ray
  He to our Northern landscape yields ?

The moon that trembles in these skies,
  Like to an argent mirror sheen —
Ruling with mistless splendour here —
  Does she above the mountains rise,
And smile upon the waters clear,
  As in my days of youth I've seen ?

O beautiful and peerless light,
  That thou should'st seem unlovely now,
That thou should'st fail to wake anew
  Those looks of heartfelt pure delight,
Which youthful Fancy upward threw,
  While gazing on thy cold, pale brow !

But this is not a kindred land,
  Nor this the old familiar stream;
And these are not the friends of youth —
  O heartless, loveless, seems this strand —
Its people lack the kindly ruth,
  The soother of life's turbid dream!

Away regret! Here must I die,
  Remote from all my soul held dear —
My grave, upon an alien shore,
  Will ne'er attract the passer-by
The lonely sleeper to deplore —
  No flower will grace the stranger's bier!

Winds of the melancholy night,
  Begin your solemn dirge and bland!
The giant clouds are gathering fast,
  The fearful moon withdraws her light —
In mournful visions of the past,
  Again I'll seek my native land!

SONG.

I LOOK on thee once more,—
  I gaze on thee and sigh,
To think how soon some hearts run o'er
  With love, and then run dry.

I need not marvel long
  That love in thee expires,
For shallowest streams have loudest song,
  Most smoke the weakest fires.

I deemed thee once sincere,—
  Once thought thy breast must be
A fountain gushing through the year
  With living love for me!

For so it was with mine,
  The well-springs of my soul
Were opened up, and streamed to thine.
  As their appointed goal.

And now they wander on,
  O'er barren sands unblest,
Since falsehood placed its seal upon
  Thy fair, but frozen, breast!

THE HUNTER'S WELL.

LIFE of this wilderness,
  Pure gushing stream,
Dear to the Summer
  Is thy murmuring!
Note of the song-bird,
  Warbling on high,
Ne'er with my spirit made
  Such harmony
As do thy deep waters,
  O'er rock, leaf, and flower,
Bubbling and babbling
  The long sunny hour!

Tongue of this desert spot,
  Spelling sweet tones,
To the mute listeners —
  Old mossy stones;

Who ranged these stones near
  Thy silver rim,
Guarding the temple
  Where rises thy hymn?
Some thirst-stricken Hunter—
  Swarth priest of the wood,
Around thee hath strewn them,
  In fond gratitude.

Orb of the green waste,
  Open and clear,
Friend of the Hunter,
  Loved of the deer;
Brilliantly breaking
  Beneath the blue sky,
Gladdening the leaflets
  That tremulous sigh;
Star of my wandering,
  Symbol of love,
Lead me to dream of
  The Fountain above!

IT DEEPLY WOUNDS THE TRUSTING HEART.

It deeply wounds the trusting heart
  That ever throbs to good,
To know that by a perverse art
  It still is misconstrued :

And thus the beauties of the field,
  The glories of the sky,
To lofty natures often yield
  Sole solace ere they die.

The things that harmless couch on earth,
  Or pierce the blue of heaven,
Have mystic reasons in their birth
  Why they should be sin-shriven.

The secrets of the human breast
  No human eye may scan;
With Him alone those secrets rest
  Who made and judgeth man.

Nor lightly should we estimate
  The Hand which rules it so,
Nor idly seek to penetrate
  What angels may not know.

Enough that with a righteous will,
  In this disjointed scene,
The upright one, through good and ill,
  Will be as he hath been.

And should a ribald multitude
  Repay with hate his love,
He still can smile : man's ways are viewed
  By Him who rules above.

THE ETTIN O' SILLARWOOD.

'O, Sillarwood! sweet Sillarwood,
Gin Sillarwood were mine,
I'd big a bouir in Sillarwood
And theik it ower wi' thyme;
At ilka door, and ilka bore,
The red, red rose, wud shine!'

It's up and sang the bonnie bird,
Upon her milk-white hand—
'I wudna lig in Sillarwood,
For all a gude Earl's land;
I wadna sing in Sillarwood,
Tho' gowden glist ilk wand!

'The wild boar rakes in Sillarwood,
The buck drives thro' the shaw,
And simmer woos the Southern wind
Thro' Sillarwood to blaw.

'Thro' Sillarwood, sweet Sillarwood,
The deer hounds run so free;
But the hunter stark of Sillarwood
An Ettin lang is he!'

'O, Sillarwood! sweet Sillarwood,'
Fair Marjorie did sing,
'On the tallest tree in Sillarwood,
That Ettin lang will hing!'

The Southern wind it blaws fu' saft,
And Sillarwood is near;
Fair Marjorie's sang in Sillarwood,
The stark hunter did hear.

He band his deer hounds in their leash,
Set his bow against a tree,
And three blasts on his horn has brocht
The wood elf to his knee.

'Gae bring to me a shapely weed,
Of silver and of gold,
Gae bring to me as stark a steed,
As ever stepped on mold;
For I maun ride frae Sillarwood
This fair maid to behold!'

The wood elf twisted sun-beams red
  Into a shapely weed,
And the tallest birk in Sillarwood
  He hewed into a steed;
And shod it wi' the burning gold
  To glance like ony glede.

The Ettin shook his bridle reins
  And merrily they rung,
For four and twenty sillar bells
  On ilka side were hung.

The Ettin rade, and better rade,
  Some thretty miles and three,
A bugle horn hung at his breast,
  A lang sword at his knee;
'I wud I met,' said the Ettin lang,
  'The maiden Marjorie!'

The Ettin rade, and better rade,
  Till he has reached her bouir,
And there he saw fair Marjorie
  As bricht as lily flouir.

'O Sillarwood! — Sweet Sillarwood! —
  Gin Sillarwood were mine,
The sleuthest hawk o' Sillarwood
  On dainty flesh wud dine!'

'Weel met, weel met,' the Ettin said,
  'For ae kiss o' that hand,
I wud na grudge my kist o' gold
  And forty fees o' land!

'Weel met, weel met,' the Ettin said,
  'For ae kiss o' that cheek,
I'll big a bower wi' precious stanes,
  The red gold sal it theik:

'Weel met, weel met,' the Ettin said,
  'For ae kiss o' thy chin,
I'll welcome thee to Sillarwood
  And a' that grows therein!'

'If ye may leese me Sillarwood
  Wi' a' that grows therein,
Ye're free to kiss my cheek,' she said,
  'Ye're free to kiss my chin—
The Knicht that hechts me Sillarwood
  My maiden thocht sal win!

'My luve I've laid on Sillarwood—
  Its bonnie aiken tree—
And gin that I hae Sillarwood
  I'll link alang wi' thee!'

Then on she put her green mantel
  Weel furred wi' minivere :
Then on she put her velvet shoon,
  The silver shining clear.

She proudly vaulted on the black —
  He bounded on the bay —
The stateliest pair that ever took
  To Sillarwood their way !

It 's up and sang the gentil bird
  On Marjorie's fair hand —
'I wudna wend to Sillarwood
  For a' its timbered land —
Nor wud I lig in Sillarwood
  Tho' gowden glist ilk wand !

'The Hunters chace thro' Sillarwood
  The playfu' herte and rae ;
Nae maiden that socht Sillarwood
  E'er back was seen to gae !'

The Ettin leuch, the Ettin sang,
  He whistled merrilie,
'If sic a bird,' he said, 'were mine,
  I 'd hing it on a tree.'

'Were I the Lady Marjorie,
  Thou hunter fair but free,
My horse's head I 'd turn about,
  And think nae mair o' thee ! '

It's on they rade, and better rade,
  They shimmered in the sun —
'T was sick and sair grew Marjorie
  Lang ere that ride was done !

Yet on they rade, and better rade,
  They neared the Cross o' stane —
The tall Knicht when he passed it by
  Felt cauld in every bane.

But on they rade, and better rade,
  It evir grew mair mirk,
O loud, loud nichered the bay steed
  As they passed Mary's Kirk !

'I'm wearie o' this eerie road,'
  Maid Marjorie did say —
'We canna weel greet Sillarwood
  Afore the set o' day !'

'It's no the sinkin' o' the sun
  That gloamins sae the ground,

The heicht it is o' Sillarwood
  That shadows a' around.'

'Methocht, Sir Knicht, broad Sillarwood
  A pleasant bield wud be,
With nuts on ilka hazel bush,
  And birds on ilka tree —
But oh! the dimness o' this wood
  Is terrible to me!'

'The trees, ye see, seem wondrous big,
  The branches wondrous braid,
Then marvel nae if sad suld be
  The path we hae to tread!'

Thick grew the air, thick grew the trees,
  Thick hung the leaves around,
And deeper did the Ettin's voice
  In the dread dimness sound —
'I think,' said Maiden Marjorie,
  'I hear a horn and hound!'

'Ye weel may hear the hound,' he said,
'Ye weel may hear the horn,
For I can hear the wild halloo
  That freichts the face o' Morn!

'The Hunters fell o' Sillarwood
Hae packs full fifty-three:
They hunt all day, they hunt all nicht,
They never bow an ee:

'The Hunters fell o' Sillarwood
Hae steeds but blude or bane:
They bear fiert maidens to a weird
Where mercy there is nane!

'And I the Laird o' Sillarwood
Hae beds baith deep and wide,
(Of clay-cauld earth) whereon to streik
A proud and dainty bride!

'Ho! look beside yon bonny birk—
The latest blink of day
Is gleamin' on a comely heap
Of freshly dug red clay;

'Richt cunning hands they were that digged
Forenent the birken tree
Where every leaf that draps, frore maid,
Will piece a shroud for thee—
It's they can lie on lily breist
As they can lie on lea!

'And they will hap thy lily breist
   Till flesh fa's aff the bane —
Nor tell thy freres how Marjorie
   To Sillarwood hath gane!

'The bed is strewed, Maid Marjorie,
   Wi' bracken and wi' brier,
And ne'er will gray cock clarion wind
   For ane that slumbers here —
Ye wedded have the Ettin stark —
   He rules the Realms of Fear!'

LIKE A WORN GRAY-HAIRED MARINER.

Like a worn gray-haired mariner whom the sea
Hath wrecked, then flung in mockery ashore,
To clamber some gaunt cliff, and list the roar
Of wave pursuing wave unceasingly;
His native land, dear home, and toil-won store
Inexorably severed from his sight;
His sole companions Hopelessness and Grief—
Who feels his day will soon be mirkest night—
Who from its close alone expects relief—
Praying life's sands, in pity, to descend
And rid him of life's burden,—So do I
Gaze on the world, and time fast surging by,
Drifting away each hope with each tried friend—
Leaving behind a waste where desolate I may die.

THE LAY OF GEOFFROI RUDEL.

WITH faltering step would I depart,
From home and friend that claimed my heart —
And the big tear would dim mine eye,
  Fixed on the scenes of early years,
  (Each spot some pleasure past endears)
And I would mingle with a sigh
The accents of the farewell lay —
But for my love that's far away!

Friends and dear native land, adieu!
In hope we part — no tears bedew
My cheek — no dark regrets alloy
  The buoyant feelings of the hour
  That leads me to my ladye's bower —
My breast throbs with a wondrous joy,
While every life-pulse seems to say —
'Haste to thy love that's far away!'

ENVIE.

Ane plante there is of the deidliest pouir
  Quhilk flourischis deeply in the hert;
Its lang rutis creip and fald outoure
  Ilka vive and breathen part:
Lustilie bourgenis the weid anon
Till hert hath rottit and lyf hath flown.

Blak is the sap of its baleful stem,
  Lyk funeral blicht its leavis do fal;
In its moistoure is quenchit luve's pure flame,
  It drappis rust on inmost saul:
Lustilie bourgenis the weid anon,
Till hert hath rottit and lyf hath flown.

Evir it flourischis meikel and hie,
  Nae stay, nae hindraunce will it bruik;
In ae nicht sprynging up, a burdlie tree,
  Schedding its bale at ae single luik:
Lustilie bourgenis the weid anon,
Till hert hath rottit and lyf hath flown.

It canna be kythit to the gudely sun,
  It pynyth sae at his nobil sicht;
It shrinkyth quyte like a thing undone
  Quhan luikit on by the blessit licht:
In hert whence heevinlie luve hath gone
Thilke evil weid aye bourgenis on.

Fell Envie's th' plant of mortal pouir
  Quhilk flourischis grenelye in the hert—
Raining the slawe and poisonous shouir
  Quhilk cankereth the vertuous part:
Black Envie wherever its seed is sawin,
Fashion is a hert like the foul Fiend's awin!

LOVE'S TOKENS.

Love's herald is not speech —
  His fear-fraught tongue is mute —
His presence is bewrayed
  By blushes deep that shoot
Athwart the conscious brow,
  And mantle on the cheek,
Then fleet for tints of snow
  Which soft confusion speak;
Thus red and white have place
By turns on true love's face.

Love vaunteth not his worth
  In gaudy, glozing phrase,
His home is not in breast
  Where thought of worldling stays;
In modest loyaltie
  His fountain doth abide;
In bosom greatly good
  The lucid pulses tide
That ebb and flow there ever,
Till soul and body sever.

Trust not the ready lip
  Whence flows the fulsome song —
True love aye gently hymns,
  False love chaunts loud and long.
Young Beauty, cherish well
  The bashful, anxious eye,
The lip that may not move,
  The breast that stills the sigh —
A recreant to thee
Their lord will never be !

O SAY NOT PURE AFFECTIONS CHANGE!

O SAY not pure affections change
When fixed they once have been,
Or that between two noble hearts
Hate e'er can intervene!

Though coldness for a while may freeze
The love-springs of the soul,
Though angry pride its sympathies
May for a time control,

Yet such estrangement cannot last—
A tone, a touch, a look,
Dissolves at once the icyness
That crisp'd affection's brook:

Again they feel the genial glow
Within the bosom burn,
And all their pent-up tenderness
With tenfold force return!

THE ROSE AND THE FAIR LILYE.

THE Earlsburn Glen is gay and green,
The Earlsburn water cleir,
And blythely blume on Earlsburn bank
The broom and eke the brier!

Twa Sisters gaed up Earlsburn glen—
Twa maidens bricht o' blee—
The tane she was the Rose sae red,
The tither the Fair Lilye!

'Ye mauna droop and dwyne, Sister'—
Said Rose to fair Lilye—
'Yer heart ye mauna brek, Sister—
For ane that's ower the sea:

'The vows we sillie maidens hear
Frae wild and wilfu' man,
Are as the words the waves wash out
When traced upon the san'!'

'I mauna think yer speech is sooth,'
Saft answered the Lilye —
'I winna dout mine ain gude Knicht
Tho' he 's ayont the sea!'

Then scornfully the Rose sae red
Spake to the pure Lilye —
'The vows he feigned at thy bouir door,
He plicht in mine to me!'

'I'll hame and spread the sheets, Sister,
And deck my bed sae hie —
The bed sae wide made for a bride,
For I think I sune sal die!

'Your wierd I sal na be, Sister,
As mine I fear ye've bin —
Your luve I wil na cross, Sister,
It were a mortal sin!'

Earlsburn Glen is green to see,
Earlsburn water cleir —
Of the siller birk in Earlsburn Wood
They framit the Maiden's bier!

There 's a lonely dame in a gudely bouir,
  She nevir lifts an ee —
That dame was ance the Rose sae red,
  She is now a pale Lilye.

A Knicht aft looks frae his turret tall,
  Where the kirk-yaird grass grows green ;
He wonne the weed and lost the flouir,
  And grief aye dims his een :

At noon of nicht, in the moonshine bricht,
  The warrior kneels in prayer —
He prays wi' his face to the auld kirk-yaird,
  And wishes he were there !

YOUNG LOVE.

It seems a dream the infant love
That tamed my truant will,
But 'twas a dream of happiness,
And I regret it still!

Its images are part of me,
A very part of mind—
Feelings and fancies beautiful
In purity combined!

Time's sunset lends a tenderer tinge
To what those feelings were,
Like the cloud-mellow'd radiance
Which evening landscapes bear:

They wedded are unto my soul,
As light is blent with heat,
Or as the hallowed confluence
Of air with odours sweet.

Though she, the spirit of that dream,
  Lacks of the loveliness
Young fancy robed her in, yet I
  May hardly love her less:

Even when as in my boyish time
  I nestled by her side,
Her ever gentle impulses
  Thorrow my being glide!

TO THE TEMPEST.

Chaunt on, ye stormy voices, loud and shrill
Your wild tumultuous melody — strip
The forest of its clothing — leave it bare,
As a deserted and world-trampled foundling!
Lash on, ye rains, and pour your tide of might
Unceasingly and strong, and blench the Earth's
Green mantle with your floods: Suddenly swell
The brawling torrent in the sleep-locked night,
That it may deluge the subjacent plain,
And spread destruction where security
Had fondly built its faith, and knelt before
The altar of its refuge — Sweep ye down
Palace and mansion, hall and lofty tower,
And creeping shed, into one common grave!

Ye lightnings that are flashing fitfully —
(Heaven's messengers) askant the lurid sky,
Burst forth in one vast sheet of whelming fire —
Pass through the furnace the base lords of earth,

With subtile fury inextinguishable —
That, purified, they may again appear
As erst they were, free of soul-searing sin
And worldly-mindedness! For mailed they be,
Obdurate all, in selfish adamant,
So rivetted, that it would need a fire
Potential as the ever-burning pit,
To overcome and melt it, so that hearts
Might beat and spirits move to chords sublime,
Tuned by the hand of the Omnipotent,
As when man, from His Hands, in His beauty came!

GOE CLEED WI' SMYLIS THE CHEEK!

Goe cleed wi' smylis the cheek,
  Goe fill wi' licht the eye —
O vain when sorrows seek
  The fontis of bliss to drie!

Quhan Hope hath pyned away,
  Quhan carke and care haif sprung,
Quhan hert hath faun a prey
  To grief that hed nae tongue;
O then it is nae tyme
  To feinzie quhat we fele,
Or wi' ane merrie chime,
  To droun the solemne peal
Quhilk ringis dreir and dul,
Quhan hert and eyne ar ful.

Nae joy is thair for me
  In lyf againe to knowe —
Nae plesuir can I see
  In its fals and fleetinge schew! —

Lyk wyld and fearful waste
  Of wavis and bollen sand,
Apperis the path I've tracit
  Inwith my natif land:
Fra it I must depairt,
And fra al quhilk hed mie hert.

Fareweil to kith and kin,
  Fareweil to luve untrew,
Fareweil to burn and lin,
  Fareweil to lift sua blew —
Fareweil to banck and brae,
  Fareweil to sang and glee —
Fareweil to pastyme gay,
  Quhilk ance delytit me —
Fareweil thou sunny strand,
Fareweil ance kinde Scotland!

Fresch flouirs beare mie frend,
  Unto mie earlie graive,
Thair bid them nevir dwyne,
  But ower mie headstane waive;
Perchance to sume they'll wake
  Remembrance o' mie dome —

And though fading, they maye make
  Less lonesum-lyk mie tombe —
Sins they will emblems be
Of thy luvinge sympathye.

Now fareweil day's dear licht —
  Now fareweil frend and fae —
Hail to the starrie nicht,
  Whair travailit saul maun gae!

THE POET'S DESTINY.

DARK is the soul of the Minstrel —
   Wayward the flash of his eye;
The voice of the proud is against him,
   The rude sons of earth pass him by.

Low is the grave of the Minstrel —
   Ungraced by the chissel of art;
Yet his name will be blazoned for ever
   On the best of all 'scutcheons — the heart!

Strong is the soul of the Minstrel —
   He rules in a realm of his own;
His world is peopled by fancies
   The noblest that ever were known.

Light is the rest of the Minstrel,
   Though heavy his lot upon earth;
From the sward that lies over his ashes
   Spring plants of a heavenly birth!

I MET WI' HER I LUVED YESTREEN.

I MET wi' her I luved yestreen,
  I met her wi' a look o' sorrow;
My leave I took o' her for aye,
  A weddit bride she 'll be the morrow!

She durst na gie ae smile to me,
  Nor drap ae word o' kindly feelin',
Yet down her cheeks the bitter tears,
  In monie a pearly bead, were stealin'.

I could na my lost luve upbraid,
  Altho' my dearest hopes were blighted,
I could na say — 'ye 're fause to me!' —
  Tho' to anither she was plighted.

Like suthfast friens whom death divides,
  In Heaven to meet, we silent parted;
Nae voice had we our griefs to speak,
  We felt sae lone and broken-hearted.

I'll hie me frae my native lan',
  Far frae thy blythesome banks o' Yarrow!
Wae's me, I canna bide to see
  My winsume luve anither's marrow!

I'll hie me to a distant lan',
  Wi' down-cast ee and life-sick bosom,
A weary waste the warld's to me,
  Sin' I hae lost that bonnie blossom!

TO THE LADY OF MY HEART.

THEY oft have told me that deceit
  Lies hid in dimpled smiles,
But eyes so chaste and lips so sweet
  Conceal not wanton wiles!

I'll trust thee, lady! — To deceive,
  Or guileful tale to speak,
Was never fashioned I believe
  The beauty of thy cheek!

Yes, I will trust the azure eye
  That thrilled me with delight,
The loving load-star of a sky
  Which erst was darkest night.

Ever, dear maid, in weal or wo,
  In gladness and in sorrow,
Hand clasped in hand, we'll forward go,
  Both eventide and morrow!

THE FAUSE LADYE.

'The water weets my toe,' she said,
  'The water weets my knee;
Haud up, Sir Knicht, my horse's head,
  If you a true luve be!'

'I luved ye weel, and luved ye lang,
  Yet grace I failed to win;
Nae trust put I in ladye's troth
  Till water weets her chin!'

'Then water weets my waist, proud lord,
  The water weets my chin;
My achin' head spins round about,
  The burn maks sik a din —
Now, help thou me, thou fearsome Knicht,
  If grace ye hope to win!'

'I mercy hope to win, high dame,
  Yet hand I've nane to gie —
The trinklin' o' a gallant's blude
  Sae sair hath blindit me!'

'Oh! help!—Oh! help!—If man ye be
Have on a woman ruth—
The waters gather round my head
And gurgle in my mouth!'

'Turn round and round, fell Margaret,
Turn round and look on me—
The pity that ye schawed yestreen
I'll fairly schaw to thee!

'Thy girdle-knife was keen and bricht—
The ribbons wondrous fine—
'Tween every knot o' them ye knit
Of kisses I had nine!

'Fond Margaret! Fause Margaret!
You kissed me cheek and chin—
Yet, when I slept, that girdle-knife
You sheathed my heart's blude in!

'Fause Margaret! Lewde Margaret!
The nicht ye bide wi' me—
The body, under trust, you slew,
My spirit weds wi' thee!'

MY AIN COUNTRIE.

Ye bonnie haughs and heather braes
Whair I hae daft youth's gladsome days,
A dream o' by-gane bliss ye be
That gars me sigh for my ain countrie !

Lang dwinin' in a fremit land
Doth feckless mak' baith heart and hand,
And starts the tear-drap to the ee
That aye was bricht in the auld countrie

Tho' Carron Brig be gray and worn,
Where I and my forebears were born,
Yet dearer is its time-touched stone
Than the halls of pride I now look on.

As music to the lingerin' ear
Were Carron's waters croonin' clear ;
They call to me, where'er I roam,
The voices o' my long-lost home !

And gin I were a wee wee bird,
Adown to licht at Randie Ford,
In Kirk O' Muir I'd close mine ee,
And fald my wings in mine ain countrie!

TO A FRIEND AT PARTING.*

Farewell, my friend! — Perchance again
I'll clasp thee to a faithful heart —
Farewell my friend! — We part in pain,
Yet we must part!

Were this memento to declare
All that the inward moods portray,
Dark boding grief were pictured there,
And wild dismay!

For thee, my fancy paints a scene
Of peace on life's remoter shore —
Thy wishes long fulfilled have been,
Or even more:

* The 'Friend at Parting' was Mr. Robert Peacock, at present (July, 1848) resident, I believe, in Germany. — K.

And when success hath crowned thy toil,
  And hope hath raised thy heart to Heaven —
Thou well mayst love the generous soil
  Where love was given.

For me, my friend, I fear there 's nought,
  In dim futurity, of gladness ;
There ever rises on my thought
  A dream of sadness :

Yet gazing upon guileless faces,
  Sunned by the light of laughing eyes,
I recreant were to own no traces
  Of social ties.

Even I may borrow from another
  The smile I fain would call my own,
Striving, with childish art, to smother
  The care unknown.

Farewell ! Farewell ! — All good attend thee —
  At home, abroad — on land, or sea —
That Heaven may evermore befriend thee,
  My prayer shall be !

Should a dark thought of him arise
  Whose parting hand thou must resign,
Let it go forth to stormy skies,
  Not tarnish thine:

Never may Melancholy's brood
  Disturb the fountain of thy joy,
Nor dusky Passion's fitful mood
  Thy peace alloy!

'Up, anchor! up!'—The mariner
  Thus hymns to the inconstant wind—
Heave not one sigh, where'er you steer,
  For me behind!

I PLUCKED THE BERRY.

I'VE plucked the berry from the bush, the brown nut from the tree,
But heart of happy little bird ne'er broken was by me;
I saw them in their curious nests, close couching, slyly peer
With their wild eyes, like glittering beads, to note if harm were near:
I passed them by, and blessed them all; I felt that it was good
To leave unmoved the creatures small whose home is in the wood.

And here, even now, above my head, a lusty rogue doth sing,
He pecks his swelling breast and neck, and trims his little wing.

He will not fly; he knows full well, while chirping on
that spray,
I would not harm him for a world, or interrupt his
lay:
Sing on, sing on, blythe bird! and fill my heart with
summer gladness,
It has been aching many a day with measures full of
sadness!

SONG.

O LICHT, licht was maid Ellen's fit—
  It left nae print behind,
Until a belted Knicht she saw
  Adown the valley wind!

And winsome was maid Ellen's cheek,
  As is the rose on brier,
Till halted at her father's yett
  A lordly cavalier.

And merrie, merrie was her sang,
  Till he knelt at her bouir—
As lark's rejoicin' in the sun,
  Her princely paramour.

But dull, dull now is Ellen's eye,
  And wan, wan is her cheek,
And slow an' heavy is her fit
  That lonesome paths would seek :

And never sang does Ellen sing
  Amang the flowers sae bricht,
Since last she saw the dancin' plume
  Of that foresworne Knicht!

TO * * * *

I NEVER dreamed that lips so sweet,
  That eyes of such a heavenly hue,
Were framed for falsehood and deceit,
  Would prove, as they have proved — untrue.

Methought if love on earth e'er shone,
  'T was in the temple of thine eyes,
And if truth's accents e'er were known,
  'T was in the music of thy sighs.

Has then thy love been all a show,
  Thy plighted truth an acted part —
Did no affection ever glow
  In the chill region of that heart?

And could'st thou seem to me to cling
  Like tendril of the clasping vine,
Yet all prove vain imagining,
  Thy soul yield no response to mine?

It has been so — so let it be —
  Rejoice, thou false one, in thy guile,
Others, perhaps, may censure thee,
  I would not dim thy fickle smile.

Farewell! — In kindness I would part,
  As once I deemed in love we met —
Farewell! — This wrong'd and bleeding heart
  Can thee Forgive, but not Forget!

THE KNIGHT'S REQUIEM.

THEY have waked the knight so meikle of might,
They have cased his corpse in oak;
There was not an eye that then was dry,
There was not a tongue that spoke.
The stout and the true lay stretched in view,
Pale and cold as the marble stone;
And the voice was still that like trumpet shrill,
Had to glory led them on;
And the deadly hand whose battle brand
Mowed down the reeling foe,
Was laid at rest on the manly breast,
That never more mought glow.

With book, and bell, and waxen light,
The mass for the dead is sung;
Thorough the night in the turret's height,
The great church-bells are rung.

Oh wo! oh wo! for those that go
  From light of life away,
Whose limbs may rest with worms unblest,
  In the damp and silent clay!

With a heavy cheer they upraised his bier,
  Naker and drum did roll;
The trumpets blew a last adieu
  To the good knight's martial soul.
With measured tread thro' the aisle they sped,
  Bearing the dead knight on,
And before the shrine of St. James the divine,
  They covered his corpse with stone:
'Twas fearful to see the strong agony
  Of men who had seldom wept,
And to hear the deep groan of each mail-clad one,
  As the lid on the coffin swept.

With many a groan, they placed that stone
  O'er the heart of the good and brave,
And many a look the tall knights took
  Of their brother soldier's grave.
Where banners stream and corslets gleam
  In fields besprent with gore,
That brother's hand and shearing brand
  In the van should wave no more:

The clarions call on one and all
  To arm and fight amain,
Would never see, in chivalry,
  Their brother's make again!

With book, and bell, and waxen light,
  The mass for the dead is sung,
And thorough the night in the turret's height,
  The great church-bells are rung.
Oh wo! oh wo! for those that go
  From the light of life away,
Whose limbs must rest with worms unblest,
  In the damp and silent clay!

THE ROCKY ISLET.

Perchance, far out at sea, thou may'st have found
Some lean, bald cliff — a lonely patch of ground,
Alien amidst the waters: — some poor Isle
Where summer blooms were never known to smile,
Or trees to yield their verdure — yet, around
That barren spot, the dimpling surges throng,
Cheering it with their low and plaintive song,
And clasping the deserted cast-away
In a most strict embrace — and all along
Its margin, rendering freely its array
Of treasured shell and coral. Thus we may
Note love in faithful woman; oft among
The rudest shocks of life's wide sea she shares
Man's lot, and more than half his burden bears
Around whose path are flowers, strewn by her tender cares.

THE PAST AND THE FUTURE.

I'VE looked, and trusted, sighed, and loved my last!
The dream hath vanished, the hot fever's past
        That parched my youth!
Though cheerless was the matin of my years,
And dim life's dawning through a vale of tears,
        Yet Hope, in ruth,
With smile persuasive, evermore would say —
'Live on, live on! — Expect Joy's summer day' —
        Vain counsel, void of truth!

Yes, to the world I've clung with fond embrace,
And each succeeding day did more efface
        Its hollow joys,
And friends died out around me every where,
And I was left to be the idle stare
        Of vagrant boys —
A land-mark on the ever-shifting tide
Of fashion, folly, impudence and pride,
        And ribald noise.

Yes, I have lived, and lived until I knew
The world ne'er alters its ungrateful hue,
　　And glance malign;
And though, at times, some chance-sown noble spirit
Its wilderness a season may inherit,
　　In want and pine,
Yet these be weeded soon, and pass away,
All unbefriended, to their funeral clay!

Array thyself for flight, my soul, nor tarry —
Thou bird of glory ne'er wert doomed to marry
　　A sphere so rude —
But to be mated with some hermit star,
O'er heaven's soft azure keeping watch afar,
　　In pulchritude:
Uplift thy pinions, seek thy resting-place,
Where kindred spirits long for thy embrace —
　　Dear brotherhood.

OH, TURN FROM ME THOSE RADIANT EYES!

Oh, turn from me those radiant eyes,
With love's dark lightning beaming,
Or veil the power that in them lies
To set the young heart dreaming!
Oh, dim their fire, or look no more,
For sure 'tis wayward folly
To make a spirit, gay before,
To droop with melancholy!

Ungen'rous victor! not in vain
Thy wild wish to subdue me —
To woo once more thy glance I'm fain,
Even should that glance undo me:
What pity that thy lips of rose
So fitted for heart healing,
Should not, with tenderest kisses, close
The wounds thine eyes are dealing!

O THINK NAE MAIR O' ME, SWEET MAY!

O THINK nae mair o' me, sweet May!
  O think nae mair o' me!
I'm but a wearied ghaist, sweet May,
  That hath a wierd to dree;
That langs to leave a warld, sweet May,
  O' eerie dull and pain,
And pines to gang the gate, sweet May,
  That its first luve hath gane!

Although the form is here, sweet May,
  The spirit is na sae;
It wanders to anither land—
  A far and lonely way.
My bower is near a ruined kirk,
  Hard by a grass-green grave,
Where, fed wi' tears, the gilliflowers
  Above a true heart wave!

Then think nae mair o' me, sweet May,
  If I had luve to gie,
It suld na need a glance but ane
  To bind me, dear, to thee.
But blossoms twa o' life's best flower
  This heart it canna bear—
It cast its leaves on Mary's grave,
  And it can bloom nae mair!

THE LOVE-LORN KNIGHT AND THE DAMSEL PITILESS.

'UPLIFT the Gonfanons of war — exalt the ruddy Rood —
Arise ye winds and bear me on against the Paynim brood!
Farewell to forest-cinctured halls, farewell to song and glee,
For toilsome march and clash of swords in glorious Galilee!
And grace to thee, haught damoisel — I ask no parting tear —
Another love may greet thee when I'm laid upon my bier!

'My bark upon the foaming flood shall bound before the gale,
Like arrow in its flight, until the Holy Land we hail;

Then firmly shall our anchors grasp the belt of Eastern land,
For planks will shrink and cordage rot ere we regain this strand ;
And welcome be the trumpet's sound, the war-steed's tramp and neigh,
And death, for Palestina's cause, in the battle's hot mellay !'

O never for that love-lorn youth did vessel cleave the seas !
The hand of death was on the lips that wooed the ocean breeze ;
They bare him to the damoisel, they laid him at her knee,
Though knight and pilgrim wept aloud — no tear dropt that ladye —
Three times she kissed the clay-cold brow of her unbidden guest,
Then took the vows at Mary's shrine, and there her ashes rest.

LOVE IN WORLDLYNESSE.

The gentle heart, the truthful love,
  Have flemed this earth and fled to Heaven —
The noblest spirits earliest prove
Not Here below, but There above,
  Is Hope no shadow — Bliss no sweven!

There was a time, old Poets say,
  When the crazed world was in its nonage,
That they who loved were loved alwaye,
With faith transparent as the day,
  But this, meseems, was fiction's coinage.

We cannot mate here as we ought,
  With laws opposed to simple feeling;
Professions are, like lutestring, bought,
And worldly ties soon breed distraught,
  To end in cold congealing!

Forms we have worshipped oft become,
  If haply they affect our passion,
Though faultless, icy cold and dumb,
Because we are not rich, like some,
  Or proud — Such is this strange world's fashion !

Rapt Fancy lends to unchaste eyes
  Ideal beauty, and on faces
Where red rose blent with lily tries
For mastery, in wanton wise,
  Bestows enchanting graces :

Yet, as we gaze, the charms decay
  That promised long with these to linger ;
Of love's delight we 're forced to say,
It melts like dreamer's wealth away,
  Which cheers the eye but mocks the finger !

And, therefore, move I calmly by
  The siren bosom softly heaving,
And mark, untouched, the tempter's sigh,
Or make response with tranquil eye —
  'Kind damsel, I am past deceiving !'

Long sued I as a man should do,
  With cheek high flushed by deep emotion —

My lady's love had no such hue,
Hard selfishness would still break through
  The glowing mask of her devotion!

No land had I — but I had health —
  No store was mine of costly raiment —
My lady glided off by stealth
To wed a lozel for his wealth —
  And this was Loyalty's repayment!

The language of the trusting heart,
  The soothfast fondness firm, but tender —
Are now to most a studied part,
A tongue assumed, a trick of art,
  Whereof no meaning can I render.

And hence I say that loyal love
  Hath flemed the Earth and fled to Heaven;
And that not Here, but There above,
Souls may love rightfully, and prove
  Hope is no shadow — Bliss no sweven!

A NIGHT VISION.

Lucina shyning in silence of the nicht;
The hevin being all full of starris bricht;
To bed I went, bot there I tuke no rest,
With hevy thocht I was so sair oppressed,
That sair I langit after dayis licht.
Of fortoun I complainit hevely,
That echo to me stude so contrarously;
And at the last, quhen I had turnyt oft
For werines, on me ane slummer soft
Came, with ane dreming and a fantesy.

Dunbar.

I HAD a vision in the depth of night —
A dream of glory — one long thrill of gladness —
A thing of strangest meaning and delight;
And yet upon my heart there came such sadness,
And dim forebodings of my after years,
That I awoke in sorrow and in tears!

There stood revealed before me a bright maid,
Clad in a white silk tunic, which displayed
The beautiful proportions of her frame;
And she did call upon me by my name —

And I did marvel at her voice, and shook
With terror, but right soon the smiling look
Of gentleness, that radiant maiden threw
From her large sparkling eyes of deepest blue,
Did reassure me. Breathless, I did gaze
Upon that lovely one, in fond amaze,
And marked her long white hair as it did flow,
With wanton dalliance, o'er the pillared snow
Of her swan-like neck; — and then my eye grew dim
With an exceeding lustre, for the slim
And gauze-wove raiment of her bosom fair,
Was somewhat ruffled by the midnight air;
And as it gently heaved, there sprung to view
Such glories underneath — such sisters two
Of rival loveliness! Oh, 'twere most vain
For fond conceit to fancy such again.
The robe she wore was broidered fetouslye
With flour and leaf of richest imagerye;
And threads of gold therein were entertwined
With quaintest needlecraft; and to my mind
It seemed, the waist of this most lovely one
Was clipped within a broad and azure zone,
Studded with strange devices — One small hand
Waved gracefully a slender ivory wand,
And with the other, ever and anon,
She shook a harp, which, as the winds sighed past,

Gave a right pleasant and bewitching tone
To each wild vagrant blast.

Meseems,
After this wondrous guise, that maiden sweet
Stood visible before me, while the beams
Of Dian pale, laughed round her little feet
With icy lustre, through the narrow pane;
And this discourse she held in merry vein;
Although methought 'twas counterfeited, and
The matter strange, that none might understand.

She told me, that the moon was in her wane—
And life was tiding on, and that the world
Was waxen old—that nature grew unkind,
And men grew selfish quite, and sore bechurled—
That Honour was a bubble of the mind—
And Virtue was a nothing undefined—
And as for Woman, She, indeed, *could claim*
A title all her own—She *had* a name
And place in Time's long chronicles, DECEIT—
And Glory was a phantom—Death a cheat!

She said I might remember her, for she
Had trifled with me in mine infancy;
And in those days, that now are long agone,
Had tended me, as if I were her own

And only offspring. When a very child,
She said, her soothing whispers oft beguiled
The achings of my heart — that in my youth,
She, too, had given me dreams of Honour, Truth,
Of Glory and of Greatness — and of Fame —
And the bright vision of a deathless name!
And she had turned my eye, with upward look,
To read the bravely star-enamelled book
Of the blue skies — and in the rolling spheres
To con strange lessons, penned in characters
Of most mysterious import — she had made
Life's thorny path to be all sown with flowers
Of diverse form and fragrance, of each shade
Of loveliness that glitters in the bowers
Of princely damoisels, — Nay, more, her hand
Had plucked the bright flowers of *another* land,
Belike of Faerye, and had woven them
Like to a chaplet, or gay diadem,
For *me* to wear in triumph — But that she
Had fostered me so long, she feared, I'd spoil
With very tenderness, nor ever be
Fit for this world's coarse drudgery and moil:
Did she not even now take leave of me,
And her protecting, loving arms uncoil
For ever and for ever, — and though late,
Now leave me to self-guidance, and to fate.

Then passed that glorious spirit, and the smile
She whilome wore fled from her beauteous cheek:
And paleness, and a troubled grief the while
Subdued her voice. — Methought I strove to speak
Some words of tender sympathy, and caught
Her small white trembling hand, but, she, distraught,
Turned her fair form away, and nearer drew
To where the clustering ivy leaves thick grew,
And shaded half the casement — There she stood,
Like a tall crystal column, in the flood
Of the fair moonshine, and right thoughtful-wise
She seemed to scan the aspect of the skies;
Sudden a tremulous tear filled either eye,
Yet fell not on her cheek, but dubiously,
Like dew gems upon a flower, hung quivering there;
And, like a love-crazed maiden, she half sang,
Half uttered mournful fancies in despair;
And indistinctly in my ear there rung
Something of years to be, — of dark, dark years,
Laden with sorrow, madness, fury, tears —
Of days that had no sunshine — and of nights
Estranged from slumber — of harsh worldly slights —
Of cruel disappointments — of a hell
That gloweth in the bosom, fierce and fell,
Which may not be extinguished — of the pains
Of journeying through lone and trackless plains

Which have no limits — and of savage faces,
That showed no trait of pity!

Then that maid
Stretched her long arms to heaven, and wept for shame;
And as upon her soul dim bodements came,
Once more, in veriest sadness, thus she said:
'I may not cheer him more! I may not breathe
Life in his wasting limbs, nor healthy fire
In his grief-sunken eye — I may not wreathe
Fresh flowers for *him* to gaze on, nor inspire
Delicious dreamings, when the paly host
Of cares and troubles weigh his spirit down,
And hopes delayed, in worse despair are lost;
Unaided, he may sink upon the path,
No hand of succour near, nor melting eye
To yield its pittance poor of sympathy;
Already, too successful have I weaved
My tiny web of folly; undeceived,
At length, he'll view its baseless fabrick pass,
Like fleeting shadows o'er the brittle glass,
Leaving no substance there; and he may curse,
With bitter malison, his too partial nurse,
And charge *her* with *his* sufferings!'

So wept
That maid, in seeming sorrow, till there fell
From her lips Grief's volume-word — Farewell!
And then, methought, she softly passed away,
As a thin mist of glory on a ray
Of purest moonshine; or like starlet bright
Sailed onward through the ocean of the night!

And then, meseems, I heard the wailing sound
Of a wind-harp afar, and voice of one
Who sung thereto a plaintive melody;
And some words reached me, but the rest were drowned
In dimest distance, and the hollow moan
Of the night-breezes fitful sweeping by;
Yet these stray words, erewhile on earth they fell,
Told Hope had pitying smiled before her last farewell.

Then all grew dark and loveless, and afar
I saw the falling down of many a star,
As the moon paled in sorrow — And the roar
Of darkly tumbling floods I heard, that dashed
Through the deep fissures of the rifted rock —
While phantoms flitted by with ghastly mock,
And jeers malign — and demons on me glar'd

Looks of infernal meaning ; then in silence
Troop'd onwards to their doom !

Starting, I broke
Sleep's leaden bonds of sorrow, and awoke,
Wondering to find my eye-balls red with tears !
And my breast heaving with sepulchral fears.

THIS IS NO SOLITUDE.

THIS is no Solitude ; these brown woods speak
  In tones most musical — this limpid river
  Chaunts a low song, to be forgotten never ! —
These my beloved companions are so meek,
So soul-sustaining, I were crazed to seek
  Again the tumult, the o'erpowering hum,
  Which of the ever busy hiving city come —
Parting us from ourselves. — Still let us breathe
  The heavenly air of contemplation here ;
  And with old trees, grey stones, and runnels clear,
Claim kindred and hold converse. He that seeth
Upon this vesper spot no loveliness,
Nor hears therein a voice of tenderness,
Calling him friend, Nature in vain would bless !

THE LONE THORN.

BENEATH the scant shade of an aged thorn,
  Silvered with age, and mossy with decay,
I stood, and there bethought me of its morn
  Of verdant lustyhood, long passed away;
Of its meridian vigour, now outworn
  By cankering years, and by the tempest's sway
Bared to the pitying glebe. — Companionless,
  Stands the gray thorn complaining to the wind —
Of all the old wood's leafy loveliness
  The sole memorial that lags behind;
Its compeers perished in their youthfulness,
  Though round the earth their roots seem'd firmly
    twined:
How sad it is to be so anchored here
As to outlive one's mates, and die without a tear!

THE SLAYNE MENSTREL.

ANE harper there was — ane harper gude —
  Cam' harpin' at the gloamin' fa' —
And he has won to the bonnie bield
  Quhilk callit is the Newtoun Ha'.

'Brume, brume on hil' — the harper sang —
  'And rose on brier are blythe to see —
I would I saw the brume sae lang,
  Quhilk cleidis the braes o' my ain countree!'

'Out on ye, out, ye prydefu' loun,
  Wi' me ye winna lig the nicht —
Hie to some bordel in borrowe toun:
  Of harpand craft I haud but licht!

'Out on ye, out, ye menstrel lewde' —
  Sayd the crewel Laird o' the Newtoun Ha' —
'Ye'll nae bide here, by blessit Rude,
  Gif harpe or lyf ye reck ava'!'

'I care na for mie lyf ane plack'—
Quoth that auld harper sturdilie—
'But this gude harpe upon mie back
Sal ne'er be fylit by ane lyk thee!'

Thou liest there, thou menstrel wicht!'
Outspak the Laird o' the Newtoun Ha'—
'For ye to death bedene are dicht,
Haif at thee here and mend thy saw!'

Alace, Alace, the harper gude
Was borne back aganis the wa',
And wi' the best o' his auld hertis blude,
They weetit hae the Newtoun Ha'!

Yet did he die wi' harpe in han',
Maist lyk ane menstrel o' degree—
There was na ane in a' the land
Might matche wi' him o' the North countree!

Erle Douglas chauncit to ryde therebye—
Ane gallant gentleman was he—
Wi' four score o' weel harnessit men,
To harrie in the South countree.

He haltit at the Newtoun Ha'—
  'Quhat novelles now, bauld Laird, hae ye?'
'It's I haif slayne a worthlesse wicht,
  Ane menstrel lewde, as you may see!'

'Now schaw to me the harper's heid,
  And schaw to me the harper' hand,
For sair I fear you've causeless spilt
  As gentil blude as in a' Scotland!'

'Kep then his heid, thou black Douglas'—
  Sayd boastfullie fase Newtoun Ha'—
'And kep his hand, thou black Douglas,
  His fingers slim his craft may schaw!'

The stout Erle vysit first the heid,
  Then neist he lukit on the hand—
'It's foul befa' ye, Newtoun Ha',
  Ye've slayne the pryde o' gude Scotland!

'Now stir ye, stir, my merrie men,
  The faggot licht, and bete the flame,
A fire sal rise o'er this buirdly bield,
  And its saulless Laird in the lowe we'll tame!'

The bleeze blew up, the bleeze clipt roun'
  The bonny towers o' the Newtoun Ha',
And evïr as armit men ran out,
  Black Douglas slewe them ane and a'.

The bleeze it roarit and wantonit roun'
  The weel-pilet wawis o' the Newtoun Ha',
And ruif and rafter, bauk and beam,
  Aneath the bauld fyris doun did fa'!

Now waly for the crewel Laird —
  As he cam loupin' through the lowe,
Erle Douglas swappit aff his heid
  And swung it at his saddil bowe!

THE MERMAIDEN.

'THE nicht is mirk, and the wind blaws schill,
And the white faem weets my bree,
And my mind misgi'es me, gay maiden,
That the land we sall never see!'
Then up and spak' the mermaiden,
And she spak' blythe and free,
'I never said to my bonnie bridegroom,
That on land we sud weddit be.

'Oh! I never said that ane erthlie priest
Our bridal blessing should gi'e,
And I never said that a landwart bouir
Should hauld my love and me.'
'And whare is that priest, my bonnie maiden,
If ane erthlie wicht is na he?'
'Oh! the wind will sough, and the sea will rair,
When weddit we twa sall be.'

'And whare is that bouir, my bonnie maiden,
If on land it sud na be?'
'Oh! my blythe bouir is low,' said the mermaiden,
'In the bonnie green howes of the sea:
My gay bouir is biggit o' the gude ships' keels,
And the banes o' the drowned at sea;
The fisch are the deer that fill my parks,
And the water waste my dourie.

'And my bouir is sklaitit wi' the big blue waves,
And paved wi' the yellow sand,
And in my chaumers grow bonnie white flowers
That never grew on land.
And have ye e'er seen, my bonnie bridegroom,
A leman on earth that wud gi'e
Aiker for aiker o' the red plough'd land,
As I'll gi'e to thee o' the sea?

'The mune will rise in half ane hour,
And the wee bright starns will schine;
Then we'll sink to my bouir, 'neath the wan water
Full fifty fathom and nine!'
A wild, wild skreich gi'ed the fey bridegroom,
And a loud, loud lauch, the bride;
For the mune raise up, and the twa sank down
Under the silver'd tide.

SONG.

He courted me in parlour, and he courted me in ha',
He courted me by Bothwell banks, amang the flowers sae sma',
He courted me wi' pearlins, wi' ribbons, and wi' rings,
He courted me wi' laces, and wi' mony mair braw things;
But O he courted best o' a' wi' his black blythesome ee,
Whilk wi' a gleam o' witcherie cuist glaumour over me.

We hied thegither to the Fair — I rade ahint my joe,
I fand his heart leap up and doun, while mine beat faint and low;
He turn'd his rosy cheek about, and then, ere I could trow,
The widdifu' o' wickedness took arles o' my mou!
Syne, when I feigned to be sair fleyed, sae pawkily as he
Bann'd the auld mare for missing fit, and thrawin him ajee.

And aye he waled the loanings lang, till we drew near
the town,
When I could hear the kimmers say — 'There rides a
comely loun!'
I turned wi' pride and keeked at him, but no as to be
seen,
And thought how dowie I wad feel, gin he made love
to Jean!
But soon the manly chiel, aff-hand, thus frankly said
to me,
'Meg, either tak me to yoursel, or set me fairly free!'

To Glasgow Green I link'd wi' him, to see the ferlies
there,
He birled his penny wi' the best — what noble could
do mair?
But ere ae fit he'd tak me hame, he cries — 'Meg, tell
me noo:
Gin ye will hae me, there's my lufe, I'll aye be leal
an' true.'
On sic an honest, loving heart how could I draw a
bar?
What could I do but tak Rab's hand, for better or for
waur?

THE LEAN LOVER.

I PACED, an easy rambler,
  Along the surf-washed shore —
And watched the noble freightage
  The swelling ocean bore.
I met a moody fellow
  Who thus discoursed his wo —
'Across the inconstant waters,
  Deceitful woman, go!

'I loved that beauteous lady —
  More truly wight ne'er loved —
I loved that high-born lady,
  My faith she long had proved:
Her troth to me she plighted
  With passion's amorous show —
Go o'er the inconstant waters,
  Ungrateful worldling, go!

'Be mine yon cliff-perched chapel
Which beetles o'er the deep;
There, like some way-worn palmer,
I'll sit me down and weep.
I'll note upon the billows
Her lessening sail of snow,
And waft across the waters —
Go, fleeting fair one, go!'

He clambered to the chapel
That toppled o'er the deep —
There, like a way-worn palmer,
He laid him down to weep:
And still I heard his wailing
Upon the strand below —
'Go o'er the inconstant waters,
Go, faithless woman, go!'

AFFECTEST THOU THE PLEASURES OF THE SHADE?

Affectest thou the pleasures of the shade,
And pastoral customs of the olden time,
When gentle shepherd piped to gentle maid
On oaten reed, his quaint and antique rhyme?
Then welcome to the green and mossy nook,
The forest dark and silver poppling brook
And flowers in fragrant indolence that blossom
On the sequestered valley's sloping bosom —
Where in the leafy halls glad strains are pealing,
The woodland songsters' amorous thoughts revealing:
Look how the morning's eager kisses wake
The clouds that guard the Orient, blushing red —
Behold heaven's phantom-chasing Sovereign shake
The golden honours of his graceful head
Above that earth his day-dawn saw so fair! —
Now damsels lithe trip lightsomely away,
To bathe their clustered brows and bosoms bare
In virgin dews of budding, balmy May!

MUSIC.

STRANGE how the mystically mingled sound
Of voices rising from these rifted rocks
And unseen valleys — whence no organ ever
Thundered harmonious its stupendous notes,
Nor pointed arch, nor low-browed darksome aisle,
Rolled back their mighty music — seems to me
An ocean vast, divinely undulating,
Where, bathed in beauty, floats the enraptured soul:
Now borne on the translucent deep, it skirts
Some dazzling bank of amaranthine flowers,
Now on a couch of odours cast supine,
It pants beneath o'erpowering redolence: —
Buoyant anon on a rejoicing surge,
It heaves, on tides tumultuous, far aloft,
Until it verges on the cope of heaven,
Whence issued, in their unity of joy,
The anthems of the earth-creating Morn:
Yielding again to an entrancing slumber,
In sweet abandonment, it glideth on

To amber caves and emerald palaces,
Where the lost Seraphs — welcomed by the main —
Their lyres suspended in their time of sorrow,
Amid the deepening glories of the flood ; —
There the rude revels of the boisterous winds
The tranquillous waves afflict not, nor dispart
The passionate clasping of their azure arms !

THE SHIP-WRECKED LOVER.

THE Port-Reeve's maid has laid her down
  Upon a restless pillow,
But wakeful thought is wandering
  Ayont the ocean billow.
Her love 's away — he 's far away —
  A world of waves asunder —
Around him now the storm may burst
  With fearful peals of thunder!

But yet — the night-wind's breath is faint,
  The night-beam entereth meekly;
But when the moon's fair face is free,
  Strange she should shine so weakly! —
Yet guided by her waning beam
  His ship must swim securely —
Beneath so fair a sky as this
  He 'll strike his haven surely!

There came a knocking to the door,
  That hour so lone and stilly;
And something to the maiden said —
  'Arise for true love Willie!'
Another knock! another still —
  Three knocks were given clearly —
Then quickly rose the Port-Reeve's maid —
  Her seaman she loved dearly!

And first she saw a streak of light,
  Like moonshine cold and paly;
And then she heard a well-known step —
  The maiden's pulse beat gaily!
She saw a light, she heard a step,
  She marked a figure slender
Across the threshold pass like thought,
  And stand in her lone chamber.

It paced the chamber once and twice,
  It crossed it three times slowly —
But when she to her Maker prayed,
  It fled like sprite unholy.
The form the vanished shadow wore
  Was of her true love Willie —
O not a breath escaped the lips
  That pallid looked and chilly!

Long motionless the maiden stood,
  In wonder, fear, and sorrow —
A tale of wreck, a tale of wo
  Was told her on the morrow !
The ship of her returning hopes
  Had sunk beneath the billow —
The ocean-shell, the ocean-weed
  Were now her lover's pillow !

HOLLO, MY FANCY!

Hollo, my Fancy! Thou art free—
Nor bolt nor shackle fetters thee!
Thy prison door is cleft in twain,
And Nature claims her child again;
Doff the base weeds of toil and strife,
And hail the world's returning life!

Up and away! 'Tis Nature's voice
Bids thee hie fieldward and rejoice;
She calls thee from unhallowed mirth
To walk with beauty o'er the earth;
Proudly she calls thee forth, and now
Prints blandest kisses on thy brow;
On lip, on cheek, on bosom bare,
She pours the balmy morning air:
The fulness of a mother's breast
Swells for thee in this gracious hour;
Up, Sluggard, up! from dreams unblest,
And let thy heart its love outpour!

Up, Sluggard, up ! all is awake
  With song and smile to welcome thee ;
The flower its timid buds would break
  Wert thou but once abroad to see !
Teeming with love, earth, ocean, air
Are musical with grateful prayer !
Each measured sound, each glorious sight,
Personifies intense delight !
The breeze that crisps the summer seas,
Or softly plains through leafy trees,
Or, on the hill-side, stoops to chase
The wild kid in its giddy race —
The breeze that, like a lover's sigh,
Of mingled fear and ecstasy,
Plays amorous over brow and cheek,
Methinks it has a voice to speak
The joys of the awakening morn —
When, on exulting pinion borne,
The lark, sole monarch of the sky,
Pours from his throat rich melody.

Hollo, my Fancy ! Fast a-field,
Aurora's face is just revealed :
Night's shadows yet have scantly sped
Midway up yonder mountain's head —
While in the valley far below,

The misty billows, ebbing, show
Where fairy isles in beauty glow ;
Delicious spots of elfin green,
Emerging from a world unseen,
Of dreams and quaintest phantasies —
Spots that would the Faerye Queen
To a very tittle please !
Away the shadowy phantoms roll,
  Up-borne by the rising breeze,
Fluttering like some banner scroll ;
  While, peering o'er the silent seas
Of yon far shore, thou may'st descry
The red glance of the Day-Star's eye !

  Hollo, my Fancy ! Let us trace
The breaking of the vestal dawn !
  Through dappled clouds, with stealthy pace,
It travels over mount and lawn.
Lacings of crimson and of gold,
Threaded and twined an hundred-fold,
Bar the far Orient, while the sea
Of molten brass appears to be.
And lo ! upon that glancing tide
Vessels of snowy whiteness glide :
Some portward, self-impelled are steering,
Some in the distance disappearing ;

And some, through mingled light and shade,
Like visions gleam — like visions fade.
Strange are these ocean mysteries!
No helmsman on the poop one sees,
No sailor nestled in the shrouds,
Singing to the passing clouds,
But let us leave old Neptune's show,
And to the dewy uplands go!
Now skyward, in a chequered crowd,
Rolls each rosy-edged cloud,
Flaunting in the upper air
Many a tabard rich and rare;
And mantling, as they onward rush,
Every hill top with a blush,
To dissolve, streak after streak,
Like rose tints on a maiden's cheek,
When, in wanton waggish folly,
The chord of love's sweet melancholy
Is rudely smitten, and the cheek
Tells tales the lip might never speak.

Hollo, my Fancy! It is good
To seek soul-soothing solitude;
To leave the city, and the mean,
Cold, abject things that crawl therein;
Flee crowded street and painted hall,

Where sin rules rampant over all ;
To roam where greenwoods thickest grow,
Where meadows spread and rivers flow,
Where mountains loom in mist, or lie
Clad in a sunshine livery ;
Wander through dingle and through dell,
Which the sweet primrose loveth well ;
And where, in every ivied cranny
Of mouldering crag, unseen by any,
Clouds of busy birds are dinning
Anthems that welcome day's beginning :
Or, like lusty shepherd groom,
Wade through seas of yellow broom ;
And, with foot elastic tread
On the shrinking floweret's head,
As it droops with dew-drops laden,
Like some tear-surcharged maiden :
Skip it, trip it deftly, till
Every flower-cup liquor spill,
And green earth grows bacchanal,
Freed from night's o'ershadowing pall ;
Or let us climb the steep, and know
How the mountain breezes blow.

Hither, brave Fancy ! Speed we on,
Like Judah's bard to Lebanon !

Every step we take, more nigh
Mounts the spirit to the sky.
Sounds of life are waxing low
As we high and higher go,
And a deeper silence given
For choice communing with heaven ;
On this eminence awhile
Rest we from our vigorous toil :
Forth our eyes, mind's scouts that be,
Cull fresh food for fantasy !
Like a map, beneath these skies,
Fair the summer landscape lies —
Sea, and sand, and brook, and tree,
Meadow broad, and sheltered lea,
Shade and sunshine intermarried,
All deliciously varied :
Goodly fields of bladed corn,
Pastures green, where neatherd's horn
Bloweth through the livelong day,
Many a rudely jocund lay :
There be rows of waving trees,
Hymning saintliest homilies
To the weary passer by,
Till his heart mount to his eye,
And his tingling feelings glow
With deep love for all below,

While his soul, in rapturous prayer,
Finds a temple everywhere.
See, each headland hath its tower,
Every nook its own love bower—
While, from every sheltered glen,
Peep the homes of rustic men;
And apart, on hillock green,
Is the hamlet's chapel seen:
Mingled elms and yews surround
Its most peaceful burial ground;
Like sentinels the old trees stand,
Guarding death's sleep-silent land.
Adown the dell a brawling burn,
With wimple manifold, doth spurn
The shining pebbles in its course,
Foaming like spur-fretted horse—
A mighty voice in puny form,
Miniature of blustering storm,
It rates each shelving crag and tree
That would abridge its liberty,
And roundly swears it will be free!
'T is even so, for now along
The plain it sweeps with softened song;
And there, in summer, morn and noon,
And eve, the village children wade,
Oft wondering if the streamlet's tune
Be by wave or pebble made;

But, unresolved of doubt, they say
Thus it tunes its pipe alway.

Wood-ward, brave Fancy! Over-head
The Sun is waxing fiery red;
No cloud is floating on the sky
To interrupt his brilliancy,
Or mar the glory of his ray
While journeying on his lucid way.
But here, within this forest chase,
We 'll wander for a fleeting space,
'Mid walks beneath whose clustering leaves
Bright noontides wane to sober eves;
And where, 'mong roots of timbers old,
Pale flowers are seen like virgins cold —
(Virgins fearful of the Sun,
Most beautiful to look upon) —
In some soft and mossy nook,
Where dwells the wanderer's eager look.
Until the Sun hath sunken down
Over the folly-haunting town,
And curious Stars are forth to peer
With frost-like brilliance, silvery clear,
From the silent firmament —
Here be our walk of sweet content.

Around is many a sturdy oak
Never scaithed by woodman's stroke;
Many a stalwart green-wood tree,
Loved of Waithman bold and free,
When the arrow at his side,
And the bow he bent with pride,
Gave the right to range at will,
And lift whate'er broad shaft might kill.
Here, belike famed Robin Hood,
Or other noble of the wood,
Clym of the Cleuch, or Adam Bell, —
Young Gandelyn that shot full well, —
Will Cloudeslie, and Little John,
Or Bertram, wight of blood and bone,
Plied their woodcraft, maugre law:
Raking through the green-wood shaw,
Bow in hand, and sword at knee,
They lived true thieves, and Waithmen free.
In the twilight of this wood —
And, awe-breathing solitude —
Heathens of majestic mind,
Might a fitting temple find
Underneath some far-spread oak,
Nature blindly to invoke.
What is groined arch to this
Mass of moveless leafiness?

What are clustered pillars to
The gnarled trunk of silvery hue,
That, Titan-like, heaves its huge form
Through centuries of change and storm,
And stands as it were planted there,
Alike for shelter and for prayer?

Hither, my jocund Fancy! Turn,
And note how Heaven's pure watchfires burn
In yonder fields of deepest blue,
Investing space with glories new!
And hark how in the bosky dell
Warbles mate-robbed Philomel!
Every sound from that glade stealing
Sadness woos with kindred feeling—
The notes of a love-broken heart
Surpass the dull appeal of art;
Here rest awhile, for every where,
On lake, lawn, tower, and forest tree,
Falleth in floods the moonshine fair—
How beautiful night's glories be!
No stir is heard upon the land,
No murmur from the sea;
The pulse of life seems at a stand
As nature quaffeth, rapturously,
From yonder ambient worlds of light,
Deep draughts of passionate delight.

Hollo, my Fancy! It is well
To ponder on the spheres above —
To bid each fount of feeling swell
Responsive to the glance of love.
See! trooping in a gladsome row,
How steadfastly these tapers glow;
And light up hill and darksome glen
To cheer the path of wand'ring men,
And eke of frolic elf and fay
That haunt the hollow hill, or play
By crystal brook, or gleaming lake,
Or dance until the green wood shake
To fits of choicest minstrelsie,
Under the cope of the witch elm-tree.
When all is hush around and above,
Then is the hour to carpe of love;
When not an eye but ours is waking,
Nor even the lightest leaflet shaking —
When, like a newly-captured bird,
The fluttering of the heart is heard;
When tears come to the eye unbidden,
And blushing cheeks are in bosom hidden!
While hand seeks softer hand, and there
Seems spell-bound by the amorous air —
When love, in very silence, finds
The tone that pleads, the pledge that binds.

Hollo, my Fancy! Whither bounding?
Go where rolling orbs are sounding,
This dull nether world astounding
With celestial symphonies;
Inhale no more the soft replies
Which gurgling rills and fountains make,
Nor feed upon the fervid sighs
Of winds that fan the reedy lake;
Leave all terrestrial harmonies
That flow for pining minstrel's sake.

Skyward, adventurous Fancy! Dare
To cleave the ocean of the air;
Soaring on thy vane-like wings
Rise o'er earth and clod-like things.
Smite the rolling clouds that bar
Thy progress to those realms afar;
Career it with the Sisters seven,
Pace it through the star-paved heaven;
Snatch Orion's baldrick, — then,
Astride, upon the Dragon, dare
To hunt the lazy-footed Bear
Around the pole and back again;
Scourge him tightly, scourge him faster,
Let the savage know his master!

And, to close the mighty feat,
Light thy lamp of brave conceit
With some grim, red-bearded star,
(Sign of Famine, Fire, and War,)
And hang it on the young moon's horn
To show how poet thought is born.

LOVE'S POTENCIE.

If men were fashioned of the stone,
  Then might they never yield to love —
But fashioned as they are, they owne
  (On earth, as in the realme above,)
That Beauty, in perfection, stil
Controls the thoughts, impels the wil.

And sure 'twere vaine to stemme the tide
  Of passion surging in the breast —
Since fierce ambition, stubborn pryde
  Have each the sovereigne power confest;
Which rolleth on, despite all staie,
Sweeping ilk prudent shifte awaye.

What though the mayden that we love
  May fail to meet the troth we bear —
Nor once its generous warmth approve,
  Nor bate one jot of our despaire —
Doth not the blind dictator say —
'Thou foolish wichte pyne on alwaie!'

We cannot read the wondrous lawes
  That knit the soul to lovelinesse;
We feel their influence, but their cause
  Remains a theme of mysticknesse—
We only know Love may not be
O'ermastered by Wil's energie.

Nor would I wish to break the dream
  Of troubled joy; that still is mine—
Albeit that the cheering gleam
  Of hope hath almost ceased to shine—
So long as Beauty light doth give,
My heart must feel, its love must live!

LIFE.

O Life! what is thy quest? — What owns this world
Of stalking shadows, fleeting phantasies,
Enjoyments substanceless — to wed the mind
To its still querulous, ever-faltering mate —
Or crib the pinion of the aspiring soul
(Upborne ever by the mystical)
To a poor nook of this sin-stricken earth,
Or sterile point of time? — The Universe,
My spirit, is thy birth-right — and thy term
Of occupance, thou river, limitless —
Eternity!

SUPERSTITION.

Dim power! by very indistinctness made
More potent, as the twilight's shade
Gives magnitude to objects mean;
Thou power, though deeply felt, unseen,
That with thy mystic, undefined,
And boundless presence, fills my mind
With unimaginable fears, and chills
My aching heart, and all its pulses stills
Into a silence deeper than the grave,
That erst throbbed quick and brave!
Wherefore, at dead of night, by some lone stream,
Dost thou, embodying its very sound
In thy own substance, seem
To speak of some lorn maiden, who hath found
Her bridal pillow deftly spread
Upon the tall reeds' rustling head,
And the long green sedges graceful sweep,
Where the otter and the wild drake sleep?

And wherefore, in the moonshine clear,
Doth her wan form appear
For ever gliding on the water's breast
As shadowy mist that hath no rest,
But wanders idly to and fro
Whithersoe'er the wavering winds may blow?

Thou mystic spirit, tell,
Why in the hollow murmurs of that bell
Which load the passing wind,
Each deep full tone but echoes to my mind
The footfall of the dead—
The almost voiceless, nameless tread,
And restless stirring to and fro of those
To whom the grave itself can never yield repose,
But whose dark, guilty sprites
Wander and wail with glowworm lights
Within the circle of the yew-tree's shade,
Until the gray cock flaps his wings,
And the dubious light of morn upsprings
O'er yonder hoar hill's dewy head?

And say, while seated under this gray arch
Where old Time oft in sooth
Hath whet his pitiless tooth,

And gnawed clean through
Its ivy and moss-velvet coat of greenest hue,
I watch the moon's swift march
Through paths of heavenly blue:
Methinks that there are eyes which gaze on me,
And jealous spirits breathing near, who be
Floating around me, or in pensive mood
Throned on some shatter'd column's ivied head,
Hymning a warning lay in solitude,
Making the silent loneness of the place
More chilly, deep, and dead,
And more befitting haunt for their aerial race?

Terribly lovely power! I ask of thee,
Wherefore so lord it o'er my phantasye,
That in the forest's moaning sound,
And in the cascade's far-off muttered noise,
And in the breeze of midnight, and the bound
And leap of ocean billows heard afar,
I still do deem these are
The whispering melodies of things that be
Immortal, viewless, formless — not of earth,
But heaven descended, and thus softly
At midnight mingling their wild mirth:
Or, when pale Dian loves to shroud

Her fair and glittering form, beneath the veil
Of watery mist or dusky fire-edged cloud,
And giant shadows sail
With stately march athwart the heaven's calm face ;
Say then, why unto me is given
A clearer vision, so that I do see
Between the limits of the earth and heaven
A bright and marvellous race —
A goodly shining company —
Flaunting in garments of unsullied snow,
That ever and anon do come and go
From star to hill-top, or green hollow glen,
And so back again ?

Those visions strange, and portents dark and wild,
That in fond childhood had a painful pleasure,
Have not, by reason's voice, been quite exiled,
But still possess their relish in full measure ;
And by a secret and consummate art
At certain times benumb my awe-struck heart —
Making it quail, but not with dastard fear,
But strange presentiment and awe severe,
With curious impertinence to pry
Behind the veil of dim futurity,
And that undying hope that we may still
Grasp at the purpose of the Eternal Will.

YE VERNAL HOURS!

Ye vernal hours, glad days that once have been!
When life was young, and hopes were budding seen!
When hearts were blythe, and eyes were glistening
bright,
And each new morn awoke to new delight;
Ye happy days that softly passed away
In boyish frolic and fantastic play!
Why have ye fled? why left no more behind,
Ye sunbright relics of my earlier years,
Than that faint music which, the viewless wind
At midnight, to the lonely wanderer bears
From sighing woods, to melt him into tears?
The bridled stream by art may backwards flow,
Youth's fires, once spent, again shall never glow;
The flower-stalk broke, each blossom must decay,
And youth, once past, for aye hath past away!

COME, THOU BRIGHT SPIRIT!

COME, thou bright spirit of the skies,
With witching harp or potent lyre,
And bid those magic notes arise
That kindle souls, and tip with fire
The prophet's lips. Begin the strain,
That like the trumpet's stirring sound
Makes the lone heart to bound
From death-like lethargy to life again,
Bracing the slackened nerve and limb,
And calling from the eye, all sunk and dim,
Unwonted fire and noble daring ;
Or wake that soothing melody
That stills the tumults of the heart despairing,
With all its many murmurings small,
Of soft and liquid sounds that be
Like to the music of a water-fall,
Heard from the farthest depths of some green wood,
In quiet moon-lit night, that stills the mood

Of painful thought, and fills the soul
With pleasant musings, such as childhood knows
When basking on some green-wood shady knoll,
And weaving garlands with the drooping boughs.
Or dost thou sing of woman — of the eye
That pierces through the heart, and wrays
Its own fond secrets by a sympathy
That scorns slow words and idle phrase?
Or of the lips that utter wondrous love,
And yet do scarcely move
Their ruby portals to emit a sound,
Or syllable a name, but round and round
Irradiate themselves with pensive smiles?
Or of the bosom, stranger to the wiles
And thoughts of worthless worldlings, which doth swell
With soft emotion underneath its cover,
And speaks unto the keen-eyed conscious lover
Thoughts, feelings, sympathies, tongue ne'er could tell?
Sing'st thou of arms — of glory in the field —
Where patriots meet in death's embrace,
To reap high honours where the clanging shield
And gleaming spear — the swayful ponderous mace,
And the shrill trumpet rings aloud its peal

Of martial music furious and strong;
Where ardent souls together throng
And struggle in the press of griding steel,
And fearful shout and battle cry,
Herald the quivering spirit's sigh,
That leaves the strife in agony,
And as it fleets away, still throws
Its stern defiance on its conquering foes,
Shrieking in wrath, not fear?

LAYS OF THE LANG BEIN RITTERS.

Among the ungarnered Poems left by the late Mr. Motherwell, I have found certain wild, romantic, and melancholy measures, fittingly enshrined in a story of Teutonic spirit and colouring, entitled 'The Doomed Nine, or the Lang Bein Ritters.' To publish the prose narrative lies not within the purpose of this selection — but the songs, which conveyed to us a very singular pleasure in days endeared to memory by the delights of friendship, may not inaptly form the concluding strains of a volume whose general aspect accords well (too well) with the Poet's cast of thought and premature departure. — K.

THE RITTERS RIDE FORTH.

'On the eastern bank of the noble Rhine stood a lofty tower, named the Ritterberg; and, in the pleasant simple days of which we speak, it was held by nine tall knights, men of huge stature and prodigious strength, whose principal amusement was knocking off the heads of the unfortunate serfs who inhabited the fruitful valleys circumjacent to their stronghold. They madly galloped over meadow and mountain, through firth and forest, blowing their large crooked hunting horns, and ever and anon uplifting their stormy voices in song.' — Motherwell.

O beautiful valley,
We scar not thy bosom;
O bright gleaming lake, we
Disturb not thy slumber;

O tall hill, whose gray head
Is weeping in heaven,
We come not to pierce thro'
Thy dim holy chambers —
We see thee and love thee,
And never will mar thee : —
O beautiful valley,
Bright lake, and tall mountain,
The Ritters ride forth !

Churls scratch, with the base share,
The flower-girdled valley ;
And sheer, with the sharp keel,
The dream-loving billow ;
They pierce to the heart of
The grand giant mountain,
And fling on the fierce flame
His pale yellow life-strings.
We come to avenge thee,
To slay the destroyer.
O beautiful valley,
Bright lake, and tall mountain,
The Ritters ride forth !

LAY OF THE BROKEN-HEARTED AND HOPE-BEREAVED MEN.

'Some of those who had been bereaved by these merciless marauders, and would not be comforted, then paced towards the hills, and looked back on the scenes of their youth. They sang with melancholy scorn and embittered passion, this querulous ditty, which later generations have remembered as the "Lay of the Broken-hearted and Hope-bereaved men," who went up to the hollowed mountain, where they shut themselves up in a cavern, building up its mouth strongly with huge stones; and there, in sunlessness and unavailing sorrow, these broken-hearted ones died.'—MOTHERWELL.

THE rude and the reckless wind,
ruthlessly strips
The leaf that last lingered on
old forest tree;
The widowed branch wails for
the love it has lost;
The parted leaf pines for
its glories foregone.
Now sereing, in sadness, and
quite broken-hearted,

It mutters mild music, and
swan-like on-fleeteth
A burden of melody,
musing of death,
To some desert spot where,
unknown and unnoted,
Its woes and its wanderings may
both find a tomb,
Far, far from the land where
it grew in its gladness,
And hung from its brave branch,
freshly and green,
Bathed in blythe dews and
soft shimmering in sunshine,
From morn until even-tide,
a beautiful joy!

DREAM OF LIFE'S EARLY DAY, FAREWELL FOR EVER.

'Others of the "Broken-hearted and Hope-bereaved men," as they went on their way, poured forth these melancholy measures.' — MOTHERWELL.

BRIGHT mornings! of beauty and bloom, that, in boyhood,
Gleamed gay with the visionings glorious of glad hope;
Dear days! that discoursed of delights never-dying,
And painted each pastime with tints of pure pleasure;
Bright days, when the heart leapt like kid o'er the mountain,
And gazed on the fair fields — one full fount of feeling —
When wood and when water, flower, blossom, and small leaf,
Were robed in a sunshine that seemed everlasting;
Ye were but a dream, and like dream have departed!
Oh! Dream of Life's early day, farewell for ever.

As the pale cloud that circled in morning the hill top,
Flitteth, in fleecy wreaths, fast in the sun-blaze;
Or, as the slim shadows steal silently over
The gray walls at noon-tide, so ghost-like on-gliding,
And leave not a line for remembrance to linger on;
So soon and so sadly have terribly perished
The joys we did muse of in youth's mildest morn;
Time spreads o'er the brow soon his pale sheaf of sorrow,
And freezes each heart-fount that whilome gushed freely;
Oh! Dream of Life's early day, farewell for ever.

The woods and the waters, the great winds of heaven,
Sound on and for ever their grand solemn symphonies;
The moon gleams with gladness, — the wakeful stars wander,
With bright eyes of beauty, that ever beam pleasure;
The sun scatters golden fire — bright rays of glory —
Till proud glows the earth, graithed in harness from heaven;
The fields flourish fragrant with summer flower blossoms;
Time robs not the earth of its brightness and braveries,
But he strips the lorn heart of the loves that it lived by.
Oh! Dream of Life's early day, farewell for ever.

We have sought for the smiles that shed sunshine
around us,
For the voices that mingled mind-music with ours;
For hearts whose roots grew where the roots of our
own grew,
While pulse sang to pulse the same lay of love-longing.
In the fair forest firth, on the wide waste of waters,
By brooks that gleam brightest, and banks that blush
bravest,
On hill and in hollow, green holm, and broad meadow,
We have sought for these loved things, but never could
find them,
We have shouted their names, and sad echoes made
answer.
Oh! Dream of Life's early day, farewell for ever.

THE RITTERS RIDE HOME.

As eagles return to their eyrie,
Gorged with the flesh of the young kid,
Even so we return from the battle —
The banquet of noble blood.
We are drunk with that ruddy wine;
We are stained with its droppings all over;
We have drunk till our full veins are bursting,
Till the vessel was drained to its dregs —
Till the tall flaggons fell from our hands,
That were wearied with ever uplifting them:
We have drank till we no longer could find
The liquor divine of heroes.
The Ritters ride home!

Ask where great glory is won?
Enquire of the desolate land;
Of the city that hath no life,
Of the bay that hath no white sail,
The land that is trenched with mad feet,

Which turned up the soil in despair;
The city is silent and fireless,
And each threshold is crowded with dry bones;
The bay glitters sheenly in sunlight,
No oar shivers now its clear mirror;
The mast of the bark is not there,
Nor the shout of the mariner bold.
But the sea-maidens know of strange men,
Beclasped in strong plaits of iron:
They know of the pale-faced and silent,
Who sleep underneath the waves,
And never shall waken again
To stride o'er the beautiful dales,
The green and the flower-studded land.
The Ritters ride home!

We have come from the strife of shields;
From the bristling of mighty spears;
From the smith-shop, where brynies were anvils,
And the hammers were long swords and axes.
We have come from the mounds of the dead,
Where hero forms lay like hewn forests;
Where rivers run red in the sun,
And the ravens of heaven were made glad!
The Ritters ride home!

The small ones of earth pass away,
As chaff they have drifted and gone.
When the angry winds rush from the North,
And sound their great trumpets of wrath,
The tempest-steeds rush forth to battle,
They plough up the earth in their course,
They hollow a grave for the dead,
As the share scoops a bed for the seed.
The Ritters ride home!

Beautiful! beautiful! beautiful!
Is the home-coming of the War-faring;
Of them who have swam on the ocean;
Of fountains that spring from great hearts.
The sunshine of glory's around them;
Their names are the burthen of songs;
Their armour and banners become
The richest adornments of halls.
The Ritters ride home!

Beautiful! beautiful! beautiful!
Sounds the home coming of the War-faring;
And their triumph-song echoes for ever
'Mid the vastness of gloomy Valhalla.
The Ritters' last home!

www.ingramcontent.com/pod-product-compliance
Lightning Source LLC
LaVergne TN
LVHW011219110826
845150LV00006B/1484
* 9 7 8 1 4 2 5 5 1 6 2 3 9 *